Vera Phillips married 'J. B.' in 1939, and also acted as his secretary for much of the time covered by the letters in this book. She still lives in their home in Dorset.

The Rev. Edwin Robertson was a close friend of J. B. Phillips and collaborated with him in the translation of *Four Prophets*. He is Minister of Heath Street Baptist Church, Hampstead, and much involved in Christian communication. Formerly he was Study Secretary of the United Bible Societies and Assistant Head of Religious Broadcasting at the BBC.

The Wounded Healer
J. B. Phillips

Vera Phillips and Edwin Robertson

TRi△NGLE

First published 1984

Triangle
SPCK
Holy Trinity Church
Marylebone Road
London NW1 4DU

283

British Library Cataloguing in Publication Data

Phillips, Vera
    The Wounded Healer.
    1. Phillips, J. B. (John Bertram)   2. Church
    of England — Clergy — Biography
    I. Title   II Robertson, Edwin
    283'.092'4   BX5199.P5/
    ISBN 0-281-04135-0

Typeset by Pioneer Associates

Printed and bound in Great Britain by
Hazell Watson & Viney Limited
Member of the BPCC Group,
Aylesbury, Bucks.

Contents

Introduction

J. B. Phillips is best known as the translator into modern English of *Letters to Young Churches,* which he subsequently extended to a translation of the whole New Testament, and four Old Testament Prophets. He also wrote several popular books of Christian apologetics, from *Your God is Too Small* to *New Testament Christianity.* Many spoke of him as the successor to C. S. Lewis. For a few years he blazed a trail with lectures, broadcasts and articles in magazines which made his name throughout the English-speaking world. Some of his books were translated into European and Asian languages.

What is less known is that throughout all this period and longer he remained a pastor, even after he had given up full time care of a parish. Through a world-wide correspondence, mostly arising from his writings, he cared for people in all kinds of trouble. Some of these letters which had come to him at a time when the authority of the New Testament was being called into question are included in the introduction to one of his latest popular works, *Ring of Truth,* a translator's testimony. He told how as he dealt with these documents which comprise the New Testament he was convinced of their 'ring of truth'. In this way he helped many to retain their faith at a time of great controversy.

But the letters associated with *Ring of Truth* were

only a tiny fragment of the hundreds of letters he received over the years and which he conscientiously dealt with. They ranged from technical questions of translation to deep questions of faith and personal integrity. His ministry was world-wide. He guided many through the dark places of doubt and loss of faith.

While he was doing this for others he was himself powerfully afflicted by dark thoughts and mental pains. He knew anxiety and depression, from which there was only temporary release. From his first curacy in Penge to the day he died — a period of fifty years — he had to cope with psychological disturbance and dark depression. He emerged, sometimes for months, only to be thrown back into the turmoil. And while he never lost his faith in God, he never ceased to struggle against mental pain.

I

The Long Struggle

On Swanage pier in the summer of 1929, the young J. B. Phillips was offered what seemed to be the perfect job. He had passed through many stages before that summer in which he was approaching the age of twenty-three. He had lost his beloved mother with a painful cancer; his father, recognizing his high intelligence, had pushed him rather too much; his step-mother had treated him insensitively. His study at Cambridge — of the classics, English literature and then (after a year of teaching) theology at Ridley Hall — had not been entirely satisfactory. But from all this he had emerged with a firm Christian faith, a convinced Evangelical with some sense of a vocation. But he saw nothing of where his future was to lead him. Presumably he would get a curacy somewhere.

The offer on Swanage pier was from the Reverend Sidney Ford, Vicar of St John's, Penge, in south-east London. Sidney Ford had acquired an excellent reputation as a dedicated pastor and moreover he was 'sound', a good conservative evangelical churchman. The young Jack Phillips could not have expected a better offer. He accepted and after ordination in 1930 he became Sidney Ford's curate.

He threw himself into his work but soon there were personal problems, a legacy of his upbringing. He seemed to find it difficult to take things lightly. Parish visiting became an intensely serious matter. His sermons involved prolonged preparation. On the surface he was a young man of high spirits and at Cambridge had had quite a reputation in this respect. He could be attracted by, and attractive to, a pretty girl. He enjoyed youth work, particularly scouting, and made a memorable impression on many of the scouts with whom he went to camp. Yet in all this a desire for perfection, which had been implanted in him in childhood, constantly plagued him and he saw all his work as inadequate.

After about three years in the parish ministry these troubles began to assume such serious proportions that on 23 August 1933, his father, who still exerted a dominating influence over him, strongly urged him to leave Penge. He resisted at first and then gradually his situation became worse. He was, in fact, genuinely ill — possibly in the early stages of appendicitis. On 9 September he told his vicar that he must leave at once. At first Sidney Ford persuaded him to stay until 1st October, but a later medical examination compelled him to leave a week earlier than that. He had no future plans, but accepted the hospitality of some generous friends at Eastbourne — Dr and Mrs Rainey and their children. The physician who had examined him had advised immediate rest, a week in bed and three months' holiday. The Raineys made that possible. After three months he left Eastbourne and was able to spend Christmas with his sister and her fiancé in the house where he had lived as a curate.

His sister, Dorothy, had returned from India where she had been a missionary teacher and she was engaged to a medical student at St Thomas's Hospital. The three of them prepared for a happy Christmas in Thicket Road, Anerley, where they were to be cared for by two middle-aged sisters who kept paying guests, and whom Jack described as 'short in stature but great in heart'. It should have been a very happy time which could have enabled Jack to plan his future career after the failure (apparent

4

only to him) of his first curacy. But he was taken ill after Christmas and it was thanks to his sister that acute appendicitis and general peritonitis was diagnosed in time. He barely survived the operation. Hovering between life and death, he had a dream which tells much of his struggle. He describes the dream fully in his autobiography, *The Price of Success*.

It was an anxiety dream in which Jack found himself trudging through the rubbish and filth of this present world. Then he was hurrying towards the alluring beauty of another world across the valley but as he approached, with great excitement and a strong desire to enter, he saw 'death's narrow stream'. It was spanned by a bridge which was guarded by a kindly figure who shook his head and sent him back to the world that disgusted him. He woke in tears to be told that he would live.

After a few days with the two sisters in Thicket Road, he went to Eastbourne to convalesce. Though physically recovered, he was still too muddled and tense about religion to contemplate returning to parish work. Dr Rainey sent him to a Harley Street specialist, who recommended that he should give up the idea of returning to parish work. This caused him great distress — 'one of life's darkest moments' he called it. It was a text in the window of the Scripture Union bookshop in Wigmore Street which saved him from total despair: 'The Lord . . . He it is that doth go before thee'.

Back in Eastbourne, Dr Rainey arranged for him to see the eminent psychiatrist, Dr Leonard Browne. It was Dr Browne who helped him to see that his problems and tensions were not religious, but had only acquired a religious form. Within a few weeks Jack was able to recognize that his root problem was his attitude to his father. He had always wanted to be, as he said, '130 per cent' and if he fell short of this impossible standard he was a failure in his own eyes. His father fixation had been transferred by his evangelical experiences with the Christian Union at Cambridge and at the Keswick Convention into the concept of a demanding God. Other pressures, too, had given his perfectionism a religious sanction. Once his fears of failure had been recognized for what they were, he quickly improved.

Nearly twenty years later he was to write, in *Your God is Too Small*:

> Of all the false gods there is probably no greater nuisance in the spiritual world than the 'god of one hundred per cent'. For he is plausible. It can so easily be argued that since God is Perfection, and since He asks the complete loyalty of His creatures, then the best way of serving, pleasing and worshipping Him is to set up absolute one-hundred-per-cent standards and see to it that we obey them. After all, did not Christ say, 'Be ye perfect'? This one-hundred-per-cent standard is a real menace . . . and it has taken the joy and spontaneity out of the Christian lives of many who dimly realize that what was meant to be a life of 'perfect freedom' has become an anxious slavery.

For a while after his breakdown Jack earned a living in journalism. Then in 1936 he received an invitation to become curate to Canon Gillingham, then Rector of St Margaret's, Lee, adjoining Blackheath. This he accepted and his persistent 'perfectionism' was satisfied by the stern demands of the rector. He seems to have continued his treatment with Leonard Browne at intervals during this time.

In some undated notes, possibly of this period, he outlines this treatment:

Psycho-analysis with Dr L. F. Browne

The Mind — will develop normally unless inhibited (given a reasonable chance will overcome ills like getting over measles).

The Will —conscious organization of all our faculties (Romans 12.1: present all your faculties to God, not 'Oh to be nothing, nothing', etc.).

Conscious organizations will be spoiled by subconscious causes — especially conceptions which *have never grown up*.

— to bring a thing into consciousness intellectually and *emotionally* is to be able to deal with it.
— unrecognized, it hampers and hinders growth and self-realization.

The Mind will produce symptoms to prevent a person reaching impossible standard. Consciously offered as an excuse, e.g., 'Oh, I could have done much better only I had a headache.'

Realize how precious success has been to me. Life was success and praise.

Clever little boy — fastidious, able to do things, quick, good at drawing, able to speak clearly, sensitive. Tremendous sense of demand.

These notes represent the kind of analysis that Leonard Browne was introducing to Jack.

After living at the Rectory for about a year Jack moved to a boarding-house where he met his future wife, Vera. Love brought heightened awareness and sensitivity but also confrontation with darkness and depression. On the one hand, he longed for a home where he could be strong and protective. His mother had died when he was quite young and part of his longing was for a mother; but he also wanted to be the perfect husband. In his love he felt joy beginning to creep back into his life; and it gave him a new motive for fighting against his depression. Once, when for two days he had passed through grim darkness, he wrote to Vera: 'I think the thought of your disappointment if I failed to battle through helped me a lot.' They were married on 19 April 1939.

Although in the first series of sessions with Leonard Browne Jack had faced up to the basic cause of his problems and tensions, he was not able to resolve them. He never doubted that his father had been a major cause of his fear of failure and he gradually acquired enough self-knowledge to deal with minor defects in his character. But the darkness returned. He began to fear criticism, he longed for praise, he could not bear to be laughed at and he confessed to himself his jealousy of those who were compared favourably with him. That may read like a list of the usual weaknesses in most young curates, but for Jack they were intolerable and debilitating. He had to do better than that.

He continued to consult Leonard Browne but the relationship that developed was also one of friendship. When he did not see Jack, Dr Browne would write to him to explain his analysis, and the correspondence continued until Dr Browne's death in 1960. Although we have none of Jack's letters, copies of some of Dr Browne's letters have been preserved, and this is most fortunate for our understanding of the development of the depression.

The earliest surviving letter is from 1940, in reply to

what appears to be an encouraging letter from Jack. The war had brought new problems, but he was happily married, living in a small flat in Blackheath. He threw himself into his work and was greatly supported by Vera. He had in fact everything he could wish for, and the ideal situation in which to work out his tensions. The war challenged and stimulated him. But that all was not yet well is clear from the letter:

> *'I am so glad you are gradually putting off the young boy with his deeds and you must just go on growing however painful it is. The pain depends on the value of the past to you. I am sure you are right to carry on on your own. That is part of the game. But I shall be glad to see you some time if you feel it would help. And don't be too proud to ask.'*

Outwardly the Reverend J. B. Phillips made excellent progress. In 1940 he became Vicar of the Church of the Good Shepherd, Lee. He was very gifted at youth work and it was at Lee that he began the translation of *Letters to Young Churches* for his youth club. But the wartime pressures wore him down, as they did many people in London, which bore the brunt of the bombing. He was offered, in 1944, a parish outside the main areas of desolation, and he left Lee for Redhill in 1945. All this time, Jack had been jotting down notes of his condition — not in the form of a regular diary but comments and thoughts about the bad times. A few dated notes before he left for Redhill show the progress of his self-analysis.

April 5th 1944 (Holy Week)
Very violent symptoms — deadlock etc.

God help me to see the negative factors operating against powers of growth.

9

August 1944
Strain of 130 per cent.

Decided it was too much, refused it without removing cause.

Result is distress because of unsatisfied demand.

Have discovered my own limitations but still feel the demand of 130 per cent.

Then the first notes after arriving in Redhill:

January 29th 1945
Very powerful negative factors, perpetrate fears, exaggerate difficulties, seem to stultify all conscious effort.

Have to *plunge in*. It must be done — 'lose life to find it'.

'Rather die than be ordinary'.

February 1945
Seems I cannot get rid of colossal fantastic demands.

April 24th 1945
The *fear* of God (so called) —

it's terrible to criticize or examine him.
Follow him and you'll never make a mistake.
He loves to bring you to heel.
He rewards you.

Why can't I drop the fantasy?
Because it is valuable, meat and drink to me — motive, reward, colour.

I just can't bear anyone to criticize me, anyone to see me fail.

My constant fear — lest someone sees through the fantasy, the little boy is betrayed.

April 19th 1945

Desperate struggle.

Discovered I genuinely believe in the Terrific Person.

The centre of my worship and energies — 'I'll show them'.

For first time discovered *real God* — was able to worship.

The God I have been looking for is not a grown-up God at all.

May 3rd 1945

Down to reality and actual doing — hell how it hurts!

I've never wanted this, dreary and pointless.

No praise, no admiration — just usefulness — How I hate just to be useful.

In the midst of this agonizing with himself, Jack wrote to Leonard Browne and had an answer at once, written on 1 May 1945:

I am so sorry to hear that you have had such an onthrust of symptoms on moving to Redhill. I expect the cause is the same as on previous occasions. The bulldog dream is interesting. The proper place for a bulldog is running freely on the ground. You are quite right — you must and can come to terms with it. Let out all these 130 per cent feelings — make them conscious — don't be ashamed of them. The bulldog can be most useful to you — unstrapped and on ground level.

One of the difficulties I had with you in the past was to get you to look without fear or shame on the terrific fantasies of perfection, etc. which lay below the surface and were making those enormous demands on you which had the effect of paralysing your efforts. I suggest that you let yourself go on paper 'in full flight' about the 130 per cent side as applied to the present situation. Never mind how shameful or conceited it sounds. It is a part of yourself and must be integrated with the rest of your personality. Have you ever tried expressing your feelings in drawing? If you let your unconscious guide you there might be some interesting results. It is rather like free association in picture instead of words. Don't set out to draw anything in particular but just what comes into your mind. Write to me and tell me how things go.

Jack was a very skilled draughtsman and he drew freely, with great imagination. His letters to his daughter abound in such drawings. Dr Browne was therefore wisely guiding him to a form of expression at which Jack knew he would do well. Dr Browne had recognized that one of Jack's root problems was shame at the unacceptable conceit revealed by his inner thoughts. This is seen in the jottings which he made almost every day throughout May:

May 3rd

I want to be colossal or soon die.

Christianity is a bore unless it can help me to demonstrate my uniqueness.

I really haven't any interest in others — unless they are connected with building up my reputation.

My reputation — that's the thing! The best vicar ever!

The fantasy won't let me go, or be used, or love other people.

All or nothing!

May 12th

Things to ask God:

1. Do you really want me to be here? Or have I made a mistake?

2. Do you want me to go forward and grow up, or are you trying to make me more dependent?

3. Is there nothing I can do to lessen the tensions?

4. May I have peace if I just let go?

May 27th
Fantastic Feelings.

I don't know why I am so marvellous — I just am.

If I left the world a great light would go out.

Much of the upholding of faith depends on me.

I can't keep it up. It's like some terrible destiny pushing me on.

I am superior to them *all*.

So they all look to me for example. I must perform properly.

May 31st
This doing — doing battle with my father.

He is the invisible Centre.

I've got to produce something to satisfy him at any given moment.

I cannot bear him to criticize.

Nearly all that I have called God is my father magnified.

The job has got to be *perfect,* not a chink anywhere.

But *if I let go* I find myself, not so weak as I thought, happy, able to work and play.

These jottings reveal a man giving free range to thoughts that he neither welcomes nor encourages in his normal life. Jack is wrestling with something that clouds his vision of God. He knows he has to clear it. The jottings were, of course, not intended for publication, but Jack did preserve them because they offered important insights into his struggle.

While this internal struggle was going on, the Reverend J. B. Phillips, Vicar of St John's, was successfully tackling a large and very difficult parish. He may have been taken out of the firing line of the bombs, of which he was never afraid anyway, but he was exposed to far greater pressures as he tried to perform 'perfectly' as vicar of so scattered a parish. Analysis of the next ten years of his life show that he made a very good job of his work.

In September he wrote again to Dr Browne and we can gather from his jottings what he wrote.

June 28th
I see now that I have never been terrific.

I was very quick as a child. I used that quickness to avoid life, to cover up my fears, to avoid responsibility.

I still want that (unattainable) condition of pleasure without responsibility.

I am *furious* about it.

Dream: managed to rescue amid the melée a baby boy, towards whom I felt a tender affection. I lifted him high above them all.

In a letter dated 7 October, Dr Browne replied to Jack's of 13 September.

I have been expecting to hear from you as to when you could come and see me again. But perhaps you want to wait a little while. I am glad that you are dreaming about your father and that in your dreams you are beginning to cope with him. You will probably get to the stage of being on equal terms with him without the necessity of fighting him.

14

During that summer Jack endured another crisis of guilt and his note for 30 September reads:

> I just couldn't bear the terrible tension and insecurity. I felt horribly guilty . . . alone . . . outcast. I had failed, disappointed, grieved him.
>
> The way of independence is the way of being ordinary — not caring for praise or blame. Containing *in myself* a just idea for performance, a reasonable standard.
>
> My security and peace of mind doesn't rest *today* on anyone's approval.

It was a curious definition of 'ordinary' and it was over the meaning of that word that he and Dr Browne had one of their disagreements early in 1946. Dr Browne wrote:

> *It is strange how you have always misunderstood my meaning of 'being ordinary'. What I mean is that an ordinary person has particular capacities as well as particular limitations, that he may not necessarily be very outstanding in anything, although he may be in some things. Your difficulty as you know has been the fantasy that you are outstanding in everything. So that what I call 'being ordinary' and what you call 'being just myself' are one and the same thing. If you are prepared to accept yourself the strain disappears.*

Meanwhile J. B. Phillips was already taking steps not to be ordinary. It is interesting that Leonard Browne in the same letter comments upon a draft of the translation which Jack had sent him:

> *I feel about what I have read that if you are writing for the man in the street literally, what might appeal to people like C. S. Lewis or me, is not necessarily suitable for the people for whom you are trying to write.*

15

We know that C. S. Lewis did like the book, but *Letters to Young Churches* which was published in the following year, reached a much wider readership than Leonard Browne thought possible. He was much nearer the mark when in the same January letter he wrote:

> *For you it is right to be someone: to have an independent judgement: to be pleased with your own work: to do things in your own way and at your own pace.*

The years of success were soon to come. Leonard Browne had said, 'Apart from the fantasy, your demand for encouragement will diminish.' Perhaps he never was apart from the fantasy, for Jack's demand for encouragement, which was really a need for assurance, did not cease. When he sent his translation of the Epistle to the Colossians to C. S. Lewis, he received that assurance, and indeed C. S. Lewis wrote to him saying, 'I hope very much you will carry out your plan of doing all the Epistles.' This work was carried out against the struggle we have been listening to in the correspondence of 1945. In February 1946, he sent a draft of part of his work to Geoffrey Bles on the recommendation of C. S. Lewis. It must have been difficult for him to submit his work for criticism in this way. But it was good — as he knew it was — and Geoffrey Bles responded quickly.

Letters to Young Churches was published in 1947 while J. B. Phillips was Vicar of St John's, Redhill. It brought him fame and some correspondence but its extraordinary success did not ease his problems. Perhaps it aggravated them. When he was showered with praise for what was the pioneer work of modern translation, and as people wrote to say that for the first time they had understood the letters of the New Testament, he jotted down his self-analysis:

16

'What I've actually done appears *as nothing* vis-a-vis the Terrific Standard.

He wrote that this Terrific Standard criticized him from inside, 'hence my unrest, irritability etc'. In his free drawing a heavy square key appeared. He commented that this indicated his failure to solve his problems. He dared not relax, lest he should discover that he was really 'hopelessly weak and feeble'. He was afraid and lonely, needing even in his success assurance that he was something. Hence his efforts to be excellent in everything and never fail and his hatred of criticism:

I feel I must be strong enough to dominate them all or terrific enough to impress them, or square them somehow, appeal, get them on my side.

And after that assertion of determined effort to win comes the awful sense of fraud:

Take away my performance and my facade of defences and I am nothing. I am frightened — do anything to feel safe.
No one shall ever see I'm afraid!
I have known, always, I think, that the whole vast effort and performance is *unreal* — it isn't real living.
Other people have got strength and real abilities.
I've only got my wits — my cleverness.
I've got so little hold on life that if I'm criticized, or fail to impress, or if for some reason the trick fails to come off, I'm *utterly lost.*
All right then, this is the game and I'll beat you all at it, even the strong ones will have to admire, and only I will know that it is only a put-up job.

The sheer honesty of these notes shocks at times, but

17

they reveal a man of true integrity. The struggle was hard and long, but such a man can retain his faith — and he did. He did not reveal all to the world, but he would not fool himself.

Apart from his translations, which eventually included the whole of the New Testament and part of the Old, he wrote a number of short books of immense influence. Before long, Macmillan, his American publisher, was celebrating the sale of the millionth copy of his books — and that was one publishing firm alone! Letters began to pour in. Readers detected a new 'guru' in J. B. Phillips. They expected him to answer all their questions and solve all their problems. With great conscientiousness he replied to every letter, and took the greatest care to understand what was really troubling the writer. There were, of course, cranks among his correspondents, but he gave everyone the benefit of the doubt. He could be harsh in devastating a false argument; gentle in nurturing a tender soul. In all things he defended the faith and he felt most angry when the faith of a 'little one' was being threatened.

All this, of course, fed his fantasies. In a sense they were becoming realities for he *was* a terrific person.

Leonard Browne continued to help him enormously to see what his problems were and to lift him out of them from time to time. In a letter of 4 November 1946 he dealt with routine psychological problems and predicted a way ahead in which Jack would soon have them under control. Jennifer was born and Dr Browne foresaw that the development of a normal family relationship would take care of a few personal problems that Jack had raised. From 1948 to 1950 he wrote repeatedly.

24 March 1948
I cannot see why you should regard your report as so melancholy, considering you are finding yourself more

and more able to cope with people and situations. You appear to be quite capable of seeing through the 'bag of tricks' and of realizing the pleasure that it gives you. Perhaps if you will realize this a bit more the feeling will trouble you less and less. I am afraid I cannot give you the magic word to reinforce your sense of humour, but I expect it is there all right (the sense of humour I mean).

2 March 1949
Of course it is the fantasy becoming more and more conscious. Now you can compare it with the facts and perhaps feel less tied by it. Don't be afraid of it. It will do much less harm when it is conscious.

21 March 1949
Having brought the fantasy into consciousness and realized it is you, and not God or your father who requires you to be terrific, you must try and get the other side of the picture. What is it that makes it so essential for you to be wonderful? With regard to what attitude you should take up, the first thing is not to be afraid of these feelings, and the second is to go on asking why you are so wonderful, and even so, why it matters so much to you. We are all wonderful in some way or another, but it is not the whole of life. The fantasy of being marvellous is compensation for the feeling of inferiority, and if you would bring out the feeling of inferiority as well I think the situation would begin to change. I hope you will just hold on and carry on.

13 July 1950
I don't think you need feel alarmed or discouraged. It is quite obvious that some of the repressed childhood feelings are coming to the surface where you will be able to sort them out and put them in their right place and give them their real value which is not the same today as

it was when you felt them originally. To me the dreams seem to be illuminating. I hope they are to you too. Your unconscious is working hard for you and I think ultimately this tyranny will work itself out. I can remember having feelings like yours as a child and they are very alarming when they appear in adult life. But you must try to see them for what they really are. I don't think you need be disturbed by lack of sexual desire. Your emotions at the moment are too preoccupied on a childhood level to allow of much in the way of sexual desire. I do sympathize and I admire the way you hold on.

29 September 1950
I am very sorry to hear that you are feeling thoroughly discouraged. I think what we have to get down to is the question as to what the value of 'bondage' is. Obviously there is some satisfaction in it to which a part of you is holding. As long as the attitude retains that value for you it is going to be very difficult for you to relax. I think the conflict is coming nearer to the surface at the present time and that is why the symptoms are more acute. It is rather difficult for me to make suggestions as to what you should do or think, for I will only tell you to think things which you say you cannot think. I suggest for instance that you think of yourself as a man in his 40s, who is entirely responsible for his own activities and not subject to the authority of a puritanical father.

Eventually Jack's success as a popular communicator led him to terminate his pastoral work in Redhill, and, on the advice of two bishops, among others, in 1955 he retired to Swanage to devote himself to writing.

Looking back on his early days in Swanage, from a time when the dark years of deep depression were coming upon him, he could see that the success had caused him great spiritual problems. He had no problem about the extra money. He had learned to be generous and was able to arrange for part of his wealth to be given to good causes and to people in need. The only trouble he had about money was a pathological dislike of paying income tax, but he was not peculiar in that! But he realized that there had been a sinister destructive element in success itself.

> The subtle corrosion of character, the unconscious changing of values and the secret monstrous growth of a vastly inflated idea of myself seeped slowly into me. Vaguely I was aware of this and, like some frightful parody of St Augustine, I prayed, 'Lord, make me humble, — but not yet'. I can still savour the sweet and gorgeous taste of it all — the warm admiration, the sense of power, of overwhelming ability, of boundless energy and never failing enthusiasm. I still do not regret it; in a sense it was inevitable, for I was still very young for my age. But it is very plain to me now why my one-man kingdom of power and glory had to stop. *(The Price of Success)*

When J. B. Phillips first went to Swanage he accepted a programme for himself which measured up to his fantasy of a 'terrific person'. He was. But even he began to see that the programme had to be kept under control. At first every invitation to speak was accepted as a challenge, as a call from the Lord. But when invitations reached three hundred a year, that theory became ridiculous. Even under control, his was a massive programme of writing, speaking, conferences, broadcasts, visits to cities and towns in America and throughout Great Britain. From 1955 to 1961 he maintained this killing programme and at last, when he was fifty-five, he cracked. As one doctor put it, he was 'scooped out'. He felt all his creative powers slipping away. He began to feel that his career as a speaker and writer was possibly at an end. He refused all invitations to speak and cancelled those he had earlier accepted. Of course, he was not finished, and several important writings came after 1961. But for Jack, the worst had happened. He felt that he had been found out — he was not really the 'terrific person' he had persuaded the world he was. All his old anxieties returned.

One of the first persons to whom he now turned for help was Dr Frank Lake, who is best known for the Clinical Theology Centre at Nottingham, with which he was associated as an honoured founder until his death in 1983. Dr Lake replied:

24 May 1961
I am sorry indeed to hear of the recurrence of the anxieties and depressive feelings. I shall be very happy to meet you and have good hopes that something can be done to meet this problem radically.

Your Letters to Young Churches *has been a* vade mecum *for many years. I have valued it because of its clear expression of the dynamic elements of the gospel, and constantly recurring theme of resources. I am quite sure that it is possible always, where a man looks to those resources, to find out the ways in which the emotional patterns and expectations of the human spirit are interrupting them.*

He then went on to suggest a meeting, which did not take place because Jack was too ill to travel. Jack seems not to have followed up the invitation, but Dr Lake wrote again the following year:

11 January 1962
I do want to say how deeply I value and am learning to

22

value more, your translations, particularly of the Pauline letters. Very frequently I use them, even at clergy gatherings, to bring home the point about God's righteousness, which delivers us in depression. The clergy ask me, 'Where did you get that superb translation?'

I am now in harness much as you are yourself. Darton, Longman & Todd have accepted half of the material I have written as the basis of a textbook on Clinical Theology. The whole purpose of what has come to be called Clinical Theology is to present the gospel to those who are, because of depression or phobia or some other emotional pressuring, unable to feel the word of God running clearly through their spirit, although, in a sense, they believe. It is an attempt to study what aspects of the word of God come relevantly and applicably to personal dynamic problems of relationships. Knowing how interested you are in all this kind of subject, both technically and personally, I wonder whether you would be interested to receive these notes, and if you would, I shall be happy to send them. If they evoked criticism on any ground whatever, I shall be delighted because this is the only way we can achieve any sort of clarity of exposition.

That our Lord does save in these states of mind and spirit, we have no doubt at all. Our difficulty is to know how to state it and make it so in personal reality.

Jack replied:

14 January 1962
If you would care to send your notes to me I should be very interested and will make such comments as I can. Having suffered from both psychological 'blocks' and the physiological after-effects of assorted virus diseases I can enter with understanding upon the subject. Thank you

for your kind enquiries. I am considerably better now but have, I think, learned more in these months of enforced leisure than in many previous months of successful activity.

That last paragraph indicated that Jack felt that he was on the way to recovery. And very soon he was at work again. His first translation from the Old Testament caused him a great deal of trouble, but the effort he made and the book's success encouraged him. For a time he felt able to tackle a new challenge, but he had a further set-back when signing copies of *Four Prophets* in the SPCK bookshop in Salisbury. His wife had to take him home, 'seized by an irrational panic at the thought of meeting people'.

He went to a psychiatric clinic as a voluntary patient and there started to write about his experience of 'breakdown'. Later he continued that writing and incorporated it in his autobiography.

The diagnosis that he was not neurotic, but simply overworked and with a virus infection, led on to the prescription of certain psychotropic drugs, but these had such serious side effects that they had to be discontinued.

Later in 1966 he wrote again to Dr Frank Lake (in exasperation and sometimes near desperation):

At sixty years of age, I have endured nearly five years of torment and fear. The reason why I am exasperated is that different doctors tell me different things. Surely to goodness I am not all that unique! There seems no end to it, and sometimes the mental pain is so great as to reduce me to helpless tears. All this means a rather restricted life for I never know whether I am going to be afflicted by a blinding migraine-like headache or by the other favourite trick of my body, a combination of gastritis and diarrhoea.

It would be easy to write these off as merely defence mechanisms but the defence against what? Most of my life I have worked hard, possibly too hard, so that I am now quite unable to relax. I have no particular problems. I am normally hopeful and like meeting people. But the incidence of disquieting symptoms is gradually changing me into someone who avoids people in any large number, and who avoids travelling far from home.

The fact that the sales of my books is over six million and continues all over the English speaking world leads me to a fairly large correspondence, but it does little to cheer me. In my own eyes unless I am doing something my sense of worth steadily decreases. In any case even if I do receive continual plaudits and encouragement, it does not seem to alter the nature of the terrors at night and the occasional panics by day.

I would not wish this letter to convey the idea that I have lost faith in God, even though I have temporarily lost my sense of him. What worries me is how much more I can stand even with prayer and all the faith and courage I can muster. At my better times I feel this is a process designed to temper and harden my character. . . . At the worst times one feels this is sheer pointless suffering and that is the hardest temptation to endure. It is not that I seriously contemplate suicide, but I can understand now what makes people take their own lives.

I have an invincible feeling, that *if* I could rest even for a few days nature would very quickly restore me to my normal health and spirits.

Frank Lake replied:

December 1966
I agree with you that perhaps the most frustrating aspect of contemporary psychiatry is the tendency, indeed almost

the invariability with which consultants disagree with one another. However, the bare bones of your story as you give it in this letter together with the feeling that you don't know how long you can last out in this fearful condition, add up to a picture with which one is fairly familiar. There is no suggestion here that relationships with parents were not reasonably good, but rather that one terrifying experience occurred within the first few months of life, which was, at that early stage, repressed and preserved within the mind. When Dr Pollitt saw you, he expressed the quite reasonable hope that since this was apparently precipitated by virus infection and overwork, the likelihood was that it would again become repressed. In many cases this is what happens, particularly if the patient tolerates tranquilizing agents. . . .

I would be interested to know whether during these attacks, you have any feeling of constriction round the head, and sense of being shut in and needing to get out of a confined space, or whether, on the other hand, the determinative experience seems to be associated with solitariness and the dread of being alone. It could be that your anxiety is determined by both these feelings.

Do you have any irrational fears, as of anything in the animal kingdom, from spiders to birds, or do you, with de Chardin, feel that there is some doubt as to whether the universe is not a mineshaft with probably no way out? I ask these questions because they would indicate, if they are present, a variety of situations which occurred within the first three or four months of your life, which have become repressed. It is for this reason that such things are so deeply repressed that they are not normally accessible in consciousness. . . .

If I were to offer you an appointment in January or February, would you be able to keep it in Nottingham?

26

Jack was unable to keep the suggested appointment, and his letter written four months later was the last of their correspondence.

7 April 1967

The irrational panics occur very much less frequently, and the sense of 'mental pain' which is almost unbearable and sometimes leads to uncontrollable weeping hardly happens at all. At the same time I am never out of pain and it is usually confined to my eyes. I don't mean that I can't see but simply that the act of seeing is extremely painful. I also get these internal upsets but not usually from any noticeable outward cause. I frequently feel sick and I am always tired, which means that travelling is a burden to me, even though nowadays my wife does most of the driving. Fortunately for me, I cannot detect any deterioration of my intellectual powers. Indeed, as you probably know, I wrote a book for Hodders called *The Ring Of Truth,* which was published last January. It has brought an enormous correspondence from many parts of the English speaking world. What appears to be happening is that the mental apparatus has been overstimulated, and I see no way of stopping it. . . .

Yesterday I did some more tape-recording and although one is never satisfied with one's own efforts I don't seriously think I am falling off in the intellectual sphere.

During this period of seeking for recovery and of suffering at the hands of many physicians, Jack was becoming more and more worried by what was happening in the communication of the gospel. This had always been his own main task and in 1959, in association with Martin Willson of the BBC, he had called a conference at Limpley Stoke. The conference members discussed some fourteen or so suggestions for better ways of communicating the message of the gospel to ordinary people, many of which were sooner or later put into practice.

Later, in 1961, a small trust, called Christian Communications Ltd, was set up to give financial help to those who are seeking to communicate the gospel. Jack put some of his royalties into this trust and it continues to this day as a very helpful source of small grants. After the publication of John Robinson's *Honest to God* broadcasters showed a great interest in the 'New Theology'. One Easter broadcast upset Jack considerably because it demythologized the New Testament to the extent of implying that the Resurrection only happened in the minds of the disciples. Jack heard of people so deeply distressed by this challenge to a faith which had sustained them all their lives that they were brought to the brink of suicide. The stream of letters coming to him now included agonizing questions about this new theology. He decided to write a new book, which he called *Ring of Truth,* to give a translator's testimony to the authenticity of the New Testament. This was published in 1967 and gave rise to another flood of letters, some of which were incorporated in an Introduction to a new edition which was required within the year.

He had not lost his touch, but neither had the depression gone away.

II

The Healer

Once J. B. Phillips had moved to Swanage in 1955, he had no pastoral care other than that of his readers. He soon discovered that his parish was now the world. Wherever his books or broadcasts went, people wrote to him. Letters came with questions either prompted directly by his writing and broadcasting, or because the writers had heard that he understood the problems of faith. Those who wrote knew nothing of his own internal struggles, but perhaps they sensed that this man had wrestled with the problems that beset so many people.

The letters were on many subjects, ranging from the nature of God to questions of translation in the New Testament.

God

Last term a fellow student and myself attended a meeting arranged by one of the University societies at which the speaker was discussing the nature of God. We both came away thinking that he had over-stressed 'the wrath of God' and forgotten that 'God is Love'. I was, therefore, very interested in reading your Making Men Whole *to find that you stress this latter quality. I would like to ask you how you link your remarks with the idea of God being a just God. It troubles me greatly how he can be both a God of love and a just God.*

He replied:

I think we must be very careful not to have a 'split' in our conception of the personality of God. You will probably remember the old story of the Scots minister who is reputed to have said, 'You must know that the Almighty often has to do in his official capacity what he would scorn to do as a private individual'! Many people try to worship a God who is less loving, less generous and less understanding than the best of human friends.

Obviously this cannot be true, as St John boldly puts it, 'God *is* love'. May I recommend you to read again the story of the Prodigal Son from Luke 15. You can see how the father allowed the son to make costly and fateful mistakes, and yet when the son 'came to himself' and returned the father made the first move towards welcome, forgiveness and reinstatement.

The real marvel of the Christian gospel is, in Paul's words, that 'God was in Christ reconciling the world unto himself not imputing their trespasses unto them'. In other words God did not reverse or waive the normal consequences of sin and wrong-doing but 'took the rap himself'.

One letter was stimulated by a sentence in his *Appointment with God*.

As far as God is concerned there is naturally not the slightest variation of his attitude towards us; it is always that of patient unremitting love. I have been impressed by your description of God's actions in Christ as demonstrating 'vulnerable love', both in this book and in others. However, I am wondering if the note of judgement must not come in somewhere, if we are to be true to Biblical revelation.

He replied:

Of course the note of judgement must be sounded, and if

you will look at chapter 6 of my little book *When God was Man,* you will see that I do not attempt to minimize the spiritual dangers of misusing this life. In *Appointment with God* I was concerned to make the Sacrament more intelligible and more attractive. People need encouragement to come to the Lord's Table far more than warning that in so coming they expose themselves to the judgement of God. At various points in my writing I have drawn attention to what excited the indignation of Christ, and what sins called forth his denunciation. I am sure that these denunciations were made in love; they were not personally splenetic, but designed to awaken his hearers to a sense of spiritual reality. If I read the New Testament aright, it seems to me that the spiritual dangers are horribly real because the universe is made that way, and not because God is in a bad temper about anything! It is in the very nature of things, it is part of the set-up, that we have to accept, 'that the wages of sin is death'. God does not judge like a magistrate, but the very processes of life as he designed them will inevitably judge people and, if they do not repent, finally condemn them. It was surely to rescue man from this sin-suffering-death complex that Christ came into the world.

If my books contain more of the love of God than of judgement, it is simply because in my pastoral experience I have met a great many people who have been made to feel guilty by forceful evangelists, and who have never begun to grasp the length and breadth and depth and height of the love of God. I feel very strongly that if more people really believed that God actually *is* love, there would be far more love and service given in return. In my judgement it is frequently the wrong people who are made to feel guilty. The insensitive don't care a damn, while many sensitive souls who read religious books are made unnecessarily afraid of judgement.

Another letter raised a question which frequently occurred:

> I have spent several years considering the remark C. S.
> Lewis has made in the Introduction to Letters to Young
> Churches to the effect that all the texts which are
> terrifying came from the mouth of our Lord, and all the
> texts on which we can base such warrant as we have for
> hoping that all men will be saved came from St Paul. I
> have followed your writings closely, and used them a
> great deal in my teaching. Your concept of a God of love
> who is in complete control of the universe is exactly what
> we need in this world of today.
>
> The problem we are faced with then is rather well
> defined — how can a God of love condone 'eternal
> punishment'? This, therefore, is the reason for my letter.
> I wondered if you felt scripturally obligated to remain
> with the traditional idea of eternal torment or punishment
> because of the words of our Lord in the gospels. My
> suggestion is that a translation which is much closer to
> the original Greek is 'age-lasting punishment' (Matthew
> 25.46). This then gives us a God such as we see pictured
> all the way through scripture. A God of justice and also a
> God of love who not only wills that all men be saved but
> will see that they are brought back into the fellowship so
> that he might become all in all.

Jack did not pretend that he knew the answer to the question, but he gave very careful guidance:

Once we are out of the time-and-space world, as we are at
physical death, words like 'eternal', 'everlasting' or even
'age-lasting' become to my mind rather meaningless. Quite
frankly I have no more idea than the next man as to what
Jesus meant by 'everlasting punishment', except that I am
sure that he could not have meant a literally infinite,

period which would seem out of all proportion to the wickedness of this little life, and would neither prove corrective nor hold out any future hope of salvation. Unending punishment seems to me to be contrary to the mind of Christ, but I could not find a word suitable for the context. Perhaps 'age-long' would do. At the same time the really terrifying part of Christ's preaching lies to me not in the idea of eternal torment, which I believe to be pointless, but in the idea that some souls may render themselves only fit for the 'rubbish heap'. We have here in this little town a perpetually burning fire in a disused quarry on the hillside and every day garbage and refuse are dumped into it. This provides a lively parallel with Gehenna of Jesus' picture language (wrongly translated 'hell' in the AV) and seems to hint at the possibility of a man putting himself so far out of the purpose of God that he is discarded as finally useless. This seems to me a frightening possibility but I would never set limits to the love and mercy of God whose will is undoubtedly that all men should be saved. Although I do not subscribe to the Roman Catholic view of Purgatory, it seems to me that the process of education and development of the soul in the next stage of existence may well prove painful to some of us. But this is a very different thing from believing in an infinity of torment.

A series of long letters came from someone as near at hand as Bournemouth. Jack took them seriously and replied at length. Two of his letters survive from that correspondence. They illustrate his patience and honest attempt to help a muddled mind:

'I am terribly sorry that my book has confused you! Who understands the nature of God, anyway? At the most we are only using highly inadequate words and symbols to describe the indescribable.

35

Although I believe we have theology as a kind of bone structure for our faith lest it degenerate into an amorphous mass of pious platitudes, I must confess that in our daily living I do not set a very high value on theology as such. For example, it is theoretically correct to say that we approach God the Father through God the Son in God the Holy Spirit. But what happens in practice? If I may quote personal experience, I have known times of direct consciousness of the 'sea' of God in which we move and have our being. I have also frequently been conscious of Christ standing by me as an almost human companion. I have also known many times when I have asked for love or compassion or courage and have experienced the reinforcing power of what I presume to be the Holy Spirit. I am not concerned to be meticulously accurate in theology, as long as my life is open to God and my will attuned to him. Therefore I would advise you, if I may, not to bother unduly about the doctrine of the Trinity, but to develop what knowledge of God you already possess by whatever means you can.

It strikes me that you may be trying too hard to understand. No Christian, least of all myself, claims to know all the answers. There is plenty of room for a reverent agnosticism over a great many issues. For example, no one really has the slightest idea why any of us are here at all, why evil is allowed to exist, or why indeed God permitted the whole vast experimental drama that we call life to be started at all! And I can think of scores of other questions which in this temporary probation-period of physical existence seem likely to be permanently unanswered. We only embark here on the mere fringes of something which will surpass our wildest dreams.

Go on believing that you live in God and God lives in you, and follow as much as you can the promptings of his

Spirit within your own. Let the big problems rest on the Creator's shoulders — where they belong. Don't try so hard; relax and be still, and there is a good chance that God will make himself more known to you as a person.

It seems to me that you have two conceptions — one of the historic Jesus and one of God's Christ. Personally I believe that these two concepts actually co-existed in the person of Jesus Christ. Obviously within the limitations of earthly life in Palestine nearly two thousand years ago we cannot expect to see the full range of God's wisdom and power, in a single human life. But I believe we can see a fair and accurate sampling of someone who is eternal, that is, beyond the time-and-space set-up. I know this is hard to believe and of course I do not press it. Nevertheless I think it is the conclusion to which you will ultimately come.

With regard to 'knowing' as opposed to 'believing', I do not mean to imply that I or any other Christian lives in a warm bath of absolute certainty all the time. I mean that when we put into practice the way of Christ in all honesty, and as we learn to tap his resources, we get a growing conviction that this is the way in which life is meant to be lived. This becomes stronger over the years, so that what begins by the leap of faith ends with the conviction practically amounting to knowledge. I have seen this happen so often that, quite apart from my own experience, I regard it as a valid piece of evidence. Further, if we read about the work of the churches throughout the world, we see that they are indeed doing 'greater works' if only because the time and opportunity available to Jesus was so limited. I believe that there are much bigger discoveries to be made in contacting the living powers of the living God, and I think we should dare to make bold experiments here. The record of the early Church shows what remarkable power is released when the Spirit of God has free access to human personality.

Jesus

For a time the book which produced the most letters was *Your God is Too Small.* These letters usually told how the reader had discovered a whole new dimension in his or her understanding of God. The book had spoken of Jack's own condition and was therefore most eloquent in speaking to those who shared his kind of upbringing. But there were also critics:

I have just been reading Your God is Too Small *and I am somewhat puzzled on two counts.*

The first is this: you say, 'No figure in history, however memorable, can possibly satisfy the mind which is seeking the living contemporary God.' You also say, 'It is of course a very big step intellectually (emotionally and morally as well, it will be found) to accept this famous figure of history as the designed focusing of God in human life.'

Can you please explain the apparent inconsistency?

The second is this: you say, 'Beauty . . . is a pointer to something beyond the present limitations of time and space.' Why do you say that beauty points to something? Surely all that we are saying when we say that something is beautiful is that we have an emotional reaction to it which is very pleasant, nice, enjoyable for us (and most other people). We admit that what is beautiful to us may not be beautiful to some other people, and vice versa.

The letter was from an Oxford college and he handled it with care:

1. I am sure that it is true that 'No figure in history. . . . can possibly satisfy the mind which is seeking the living . . . God'. The point I was trying to make is that if Jesus were only a figure in history he would indeed be memorable and admirable but could not satisfy contemporary needs. But in my experience and in that of thousands of others he becomes a living figure, active and potent in the world today, once one makes the act of what is commonly called faith. Yet it remains true that the focusing of God in Jesus 1900 years ago can be no more than a partial, even though perfectly authentic, revelation of God's character. It is the Spirit of Jesus as revealed in his short and rather limited life which gives us a clue to the nature of human living. And many find by experience that this Spirit is equally alive today.

2. Here, of course, we enter the aesthetic and philosophical field on which I can only report the results of observation and experience. It does not particularly matter whether one man's meat is another man's poison in art, surely. The point really is that all true art loosens for the time the bonds of man's mortality and brings him, sometimes with a great sadness or even nosatalgia, into contact with a dimension far beyond his present restricted living. I would say that our reaction to beautiful things goes far beyond producing a 'pleasant, nice and enjoyable' reaction. You may think me old-fashioned but I take the view that the true artist is interpreting something of eternal beauty and truth — a Platonic view of course. Some modern artists, though not all, are doing no more than revealing their own ingrowing conflicts and reactions. They are not pointers to anything but the artist's personality, which may or may not be interesting. I still think that Browning's 'sunset touch' etc. in *Bishop*

Blougram's Apology is a perfectly valid argument to any mind that had not been over-conditioned by a scientific upbringing. Obviously you may not agree with my argument, but I hope you will agree that I had reason in my own sight for writing what I wrote.

The care he showed in dealing with personal problems comes out very clearly in a series of letters to a correspondent who had written with questions about the cursing of the fig tree (Matthew 21.19) and the sinlessness of Jesus.

I certainly appreciate your difficulty about the cursing of the barren fig-tree, which I must confess has always seemed to me a very odd incident. But I do think we must remember that the life of Jesus was recorded by human beings who may easily have misinterpreted some of his sayings and doings. The Gospel of Mark, which is the earliest, was probably written in 65, more than thirty years after the death of Jesus. It seems to me quite possible that a small amount of error may have crept in here and there, although I am thoroughly convinced of the substantial accuracy of the Gospel records. Let us remember too that the Gospels are very economically worded, using the minimum of adverbs and adjectives. There is often no hint as to *how* a certain remark was made. I have always imagined, for example, that Jesus' apparently stern reply to the Syrophoenician woman was made with a twinkle in the eye, even though the actual wording sounded severe. Or they could have been spoken musingly or teasingly. There is nothing in the records to tell the manner of his speaking. But surely we must never allow isolated instances to contradict the total impact of his matchless personality.

Now to return to the fig-tree. Let us use a little

imaginative sympathy. Jesus, though the Son of God, was completely human. He was not immune from strain, weariness, disappointment or horror. At the time at which he is reported to have cursed the fig-tree I think that the full dreadfulness of what was going to happen to him was beginning to close over his spirit. Terrible enough for us to see the Son of God rejected, but how infinitely more so for this man with his far deeper insight, far greater sensitiveness. We have all known what it is to be so *distrait* that we 'hardly knew what we were doing'. I find it not impossible to imagine that such was Jesus' mental and spiritual distress that even he in his perfect humanity hardly knew what he was doing. Later, when his action was questioned by the disciples, his reply about faith is almost unbearable in its bitterness. I wonder if you can follow me here. If not, why not just remove the incident, which is not of fundamental importance, altogether from your mind? It *may* be a piece of misreporting, it may even be an error which has somehow crept in. But nevertheless do remember always the full humanity of Jesus; he was never God *pretending* to be Man! Think of his real agony in the Garden of Gethsemane, think of the state of mind he must have been in when he told his disciples to sell their clothes and buy swords, and then almost as quickly withdraw the suggestion. Here, to my mind, is no plaster saint but a real man, with real emotions, which he had to contend with, with the help of his Father, just as we do.

She was not completely satisfied, but Jack persisted with another letter.

All that Christians claim is that the character of Christ is an accurate reproduction in human terms of God's own character. But plainly certain God-like characteristics had to be laid aside. Jesus was neither omniscient,

41

omnipotent, nor omni-present. He was plainly limited by the intellectual outlook of his time, and this kind of willing self-limitation is surely what Paul meant in Philippians 2.6—8. Christ deliberately laid aside the privileges and prerogatives of power in order that he might live as a normal human being. His sinlessness sprang not from a built-in perfection, but from a perfect co-operation with the Father's will. It was not that he was not able to sin, but that he was able not to sin.

Anyway, if I may advise you, I should admire and reverence what I can, and pray that I may see more. I am sure that with your honest outlook and determination to get at the truth of things, you will not be disappointed.

God be with you.

The volume of correspondence became so great that he had to classify the questions and concerns. By drafting letters on specific points which kept recurring he was able to reduce his work load.

One of these drafts concerned the nature of Christ as God and Man:

1. The Gospels are not biographies in the modern sense. They are collected 'Sayings of Jesus' and were put together by various people at different times. We have to remember that no history as we know it was written in the ancient world. Even the works of Thucydides, the Greek historian, and Julius Caesar's own account of his war in Gaul, were composed to suit the subject matter. This does not mean that the Gospel material is unreliable but simply that our modern method of reporting events as they happened did not exist.

2. The oriental memory is particularly retentive, as many of my friends who have lived in Eastern countries have assured me. In the first days of the Church there seemed

little need of written books or scrolls and it was only as the first generation of Christians died off that the New Testament came to be committed to writing for distribution in scattered local churches.

3. It would appear that Luke, who was a physician and plainly a lover of human beings, took the trouble to verify his facts and, quite possibly, was the first of our modern interviewers. Thus we owe to his research the parable of the Prodigal Son and the walk to Emmaus and much beside. He himself states this in his preamble at the beginning of his Gospel.

4. I think we need at all times to remember that Jesus was fully human as well as the son of God. He would therefore share many of the beliefs and expressions of the Jewish people among whom he had been educated. Thus he would use the story of Jonah or Lot's wife as ready-made examples already existing in the minds of his hearers.

Incidentally neither the Greek of the New Testament nor the Hebrew of the Old Testament talks of a 'whale' but of a 'sea-monster'. I have read well-attested stories of people who have been swallowed and vomited up again by such creatures, but it doesn't really matter whether one regards this story or that of Lot's wife as actual history or myth with a meaning.

5. Even if we suppose that Jesus in his earthly form was perfect in his scientific and historical knowledge, he nevertheless very commonly used the *argumentum ad hominem* method. We frequently do this when dealing with children or the less-educated adult. We use the knowledge that they have in order to lead them on to something that they do not yet know.

6. Again, I think we should remember at all times two important factors viz. (a) Jesus normally spoke in Aramaic and what we are reading is Greek and thus we lose certain nuances, and (b) although I personally believe in the basic historic reliability of the Gospels they are not chronologically arranged nor set out as we might do today to make a good story. In fact the eye-witnesses could do no more than record what their limited outlook would permit. Again and again I get the impression that they scarcely appreciated *at the time* who Jesus really was and indeed is. He promised them the Spirit who would lead them into all truth and to me that means not merely the early disciples but all honest followers of Christ today. We are not living in the first century AD and we have to be alert and sensitive to the guiding of the Spirit of Jesus Christ in today's perplexing world.

The Gospels

Letters came from distant places, including a long letter from an army Major in Oman. It dealt somewhat critically with *New Testament Christianity* and the question of hell-fire preaching came up, as it frequently did. Jack received the criticism courteously and used all his experience of translating to put over his views:

I would assure you that my 'Church' is not too small! Indeed I would include in what I consider to be the Church many who are following in the way of Christ unwittingly. I believe with all my heart, 'Every one that loveth is born of God and knoweth God' (1 John 4.7). The real spiritual danger is surely from those who do not love or who cannot love or have sinned away their capacity to love. This seems to me to be true both to Scripture and

44

to experience, and is only common sense if it is true that God is love.

The reason why I object to methods of guilt-injection is because in pastoral work I had to deal with people who had been frightened into states of unnatural guilt by unscrupulous evangelists. But there is a basic misconception here. The 'hell-fire' which Jesus sometimes spoke of is a translation of a Hebrew word *Gehenna*. Metaphorically Jesus uses the figure of *Gehenna* to mean 'celestial rubbish dump', and the consequence of certain courses of action is not everlasting torture but destruction as useless and dangerous rubbish. Jesus certainly used the weapon of fear against the cosily complacent, but very rarely against the ordinary run of sinners.

As a matter of personal history it might interest you to know that I conducted a Mission at an USAF Base in Suffolk not long ago. I preached Christ and his way of life without any threat of hell-fire. Nevertheless, as I expected, the Holy Spirit himself convicted men of their need and their sins. But no one was driven round the bend by an artificially induced sense of sin. My wrath against those who produce such a false sense is based on experience; it makes my blood boil to see how the emotionally tough evangelist can misuse his power in such a disgusting way.

Letters continued to arrive objecting to some references in *New Testament Christianity* which seemed to disparage modern evangelists.

There were also many who thought he made the gospel too much a gospel without judgement — too much a gospel of love! To one such letter he replied:

The methods of Jesus himself do indeed need to be studied most carefully. For example, Nicodemus, the highly religious man, was told that he must be 'born again' before he could even see the Kingdom of God. But Levi was called by a simple 'Follow me'. When the risen Christ met Paul on the road to Damascus he did not speak a single word of reproach, despite the really terrible damage Saul had done to the Church but simply asked a very pointed question. But evangelicals, generally speaking, have got their thinking muddled and will apply what was said to one man as being of universal application. Jesus spoke the truth in love, and that meant the most scathing denunciations of those who thought they were 'saved' and certain of their own salvation. And so one could go on; the variety is enormous and should, I repeat, be studied by all evangelists. I am well aware I shall not change your views, but I think I might as well make my own position clear. Jesus was, I believe, God himself appearing in human life as a human being. He alone could dare to say with complete authority, 'It was said to you of old time . . . *but* I say unto you . . .' People don't seem to realize what a revolutionary teacher Jesus was, or how his conceptions of the Kingdom superseded and outmoded the ideas which went before. If this were not so, why did he himself declare that the least member of the Kingdom is greater than John the Baptist?

Although he was an evangelical and frequently conducted Missions, Jack remained troubled by the techniques of modern evangelists. This he expressed publicly — even daring to criticize Billy Graham on this score — although he liked and admired Billy.

In a typical answer to those puzzled by his attitude he says:

The reason why I have attacked modern techniques of guilt injection is because I have seen tragic results in the personalities of people vulnerable to this kind of attack. (I protested against this sort of thing in books I wrote long before I had ever heard of Billy Graham.)

It is exactly the same technique as Communist brain-washing, and it is noticeably absent in the New Testament. When Billy Graham was in this country the real tough eggs never went near his meetings, but a great many nice kindly people with sensitive consciences were made to feel quite unnecessarily miserable.

I suggest you read the New Testament with a more open mind.

A long letter from a school in Yorkshire, which discussed the problem of teaching Jesus to children, called forth his sympathy and he spent much time on the topic nearest to his heart — the communication of the gospel to the young. We quote his reply:

1. After attending many meetings of sixth-formers, students and the like, I am quite sure that an intelligent presentation of Christianity will always secure the deepest attention. Would that we had more people of unquestioned intellectual calibre who would put out honest fact-finding Christian writing! There is no need to be intellectually dishonest in being a Christian, and in fact the deeper one goes in thought into the significance of what we commonly call the 'incarnation' the more one can see it as a key to more and more insights into human problems.

2. I am an unorthodox parson, and I sometimes think it is much more important for young children to grow up in a Christian atmosphere, i.e., one of love, forbearance, fair-play and consideration for other people, than for them to be familiar with the Bible. I know that I suffered myself from far too much emotional stimulus in religious matters in my tenderest years, and I am determined that the same thing shall not happen to my daughter. Naturally

47

she receives Scripture lessons at school, and comes to church once a Sunday during the holidays. I doubt if she gets very much out of this public worship, but at least she realizes unconsciously that quite a lot of people do in fact worship Sunday by Sunday.

3. In teaching myself at children's church or in church day school, I have always tried to emphasize the fact that we're not alone on this little planet because God has actually visited it in the person of Jesus Christ. I have mostly found that children can more or less appreciate that the character that they see in Jesus is the same as the character of the great fatherly wisdom who rules this amazing universe. With young children I have never dwelt on the horrors of the crucifixion, but stressed the resounding triumph of the resurrection. I don't think it is ever right to teach children about Christ's death without at least some hint of the triumphant ending of the story.

4. I am afraid I am rather naughty about the Old Testament. From pastoral experience I would say more wrong ideas of God come from the Old Testament than from any other single source! I can only say that it must require very great skill to communicate the essential message of the Prophets, for example, to any but the most intelligent of children. The whole Old Testament world is so remote in almost every particular from this jet and space-age that I cannot be surprized when I find children bored with it. But properly presented, the idea that God himself has actually visited this little floating ball can be immensely exciting!

The Bible

A great deal of Jack's correspondence related to his translations of the New Testament. Even in the 1960s there were many who were still resentful of modern translations, regarding them as a slight on the beloved Authorized Version. They wrote to J. B. Phillips accusing him of sacrilege.

One correspondent reacted angrily to his *Church Times* article because he had written '. . . there are millions of people today to whom it (the AV) is largely unintelligible'. She had heard and read the statement so often, she wrote, that she challenged him to prove it. She got more than she bargained for in a long and carefully considered letter:

1. 'There are millions of people today to whom it (the AV) is largely unintelligible.' This you say is 'an unconsidered statement'. So far from being unconsidered, it is a very deliberate conclusion from experience over many years. The sole reason why I began to translate in 1941 was because the young Londoners in my charge found the AV unintelligible.

2. You say, 'To those of us brought up in the Christian Faith, it is not unintelligible'. Quite so, but whoever said it was? The point is that well over ninety per cent of people in this country are in no way 'brought up in the Christian Faith'. They are also souls for whom Christ died, and if the rendering of archaic words into modern words sets free God's truth for them, what Christian could object?

3. You seem to assume that modern translators like myself are somehow against the AV. This is not true. I doubt if its majesty of language will be equalled still less surpassed. But will you consider this: every week of my life I receive letters from all over the English speaking world, from elderly people as well as from young people,

saying in effect, 'Now at last the Bible makes sense to me.' My work is not a 'stunt', but a careful and prayerful piece of work which has stretched my mental and spiritual capacities to the utmost. I am thankful to God that well over three and a half million people have bought my translational work, and that letters continue to flow in showing what illumination it has brought. Of course I do not take personal credit for this; I did not write Holy Scripture! But I am thankful to God that I was inspired to undertake and carry through an arduous task which has obviously proved profitable.

4. You are mistaken in thinking that there are only a few archaisms in the AV and in the Prayer Book. There are literally dozens of them. 'Let' has changed its meaning entirely, and so has 'prevent', 'communicate', 'conversation', 'comprehend', 'wealth', 'allege', 'demand', and a great many more.

It would appear that you have not read my Introduction to my *New Testament in Modern English,* or C. S. Lewis's Introduction to my *Letters to Young Churches.* Both of these might convince you of the absolute necessity for modern translation in our day and age.

Others were even more forthright. A blast of criticism for his translation, typical of many he received, came from South Wales:

Will you be kind enough to tell us who gave you the authority to violate and trifle with the Sacred Word of GOD. There is only one translation of the Bible and that is the Authorized Version; The King James Version, and any other copies are Sacrilege and an insult to simple, humble folk such as myself. To listen to some of you fellows reading over the air is painful and pathetic with your impudent and arrogant suggestions that the Bible is

50

*out of date, no longer accommodating, incomprehensible,
should be easy reading and so on, there is nothing easy
about the Gospel of Jesus Christ of Nazareth . . . .'*
P.S. *I regret that I am not a member of any church but I
do like to hear the reading of the Bible.*

Jack answered with the authority of experience and a
deep love for the Authorized Version:

> You are not alone in admiring the beauty and majesty of
> the Authorized Version of the Bible. But, as I am sure
> you must know, the Old Testament was originally written
> in Hebrew, and the New Testament in Greek. Conse-
> quently translations into different languages have had to
> be made over the centuries, and as the gospel of Christ
> goes further afield, further translations, even today, have
> to be made by patient and devoted servants of the Lord.
> Their aim, as is the aim of every translator, is to make the
> Word of God intelligible in their own language to people
> for whom Christ died.
>
> We are fortunate in England that we were given some
> sixteen hundred years after Christ a truly beautiful version
> of the Bible. Modern translators such as myself are not
> condemning this version, but are simply trying to make
> clear to people the essential Word of God. I do not think
> you would write as you do if you knew how God himself
> has blessed the work of hundreds of translators through-
> out the years. No reputable translator wishes to alter or
> dilute the truth of God; he only wants to make it clear.

A letter inviting him to speak at an army camp, one of
the many invitations he had to decline, raised the question
of fundamentalism and also seemed to commend a
rational approach to the Bible — possibly even a
rationalistic approach, which Jack was at pains to refute.
He answered warily, because he had himself felt the

attraction of a certain kind of rigid unquestioning faith he had seen in others. He rejected it for himself without moving to a liberal position. Out of his experience came very wise advice:

What is wrong with fundamentalism is that it assumes that all truth is contained within the Bible and does not recognize the many paths along which the wisdom of God may come into human life. Further, fundamentalists usually hold a theory of 'verbal inspiration' of the Scriptures which is quite untenable for two reasons:

(a) In no case has God permitted the original writing of any book of the Bible to survive, and even the most reliable copies show some divergence in detail. Personally I think this is a good thing since it prevents us from worshipping the Book instead of the God who inspired it. In any case, we're not guaranteed infallibility by either Pope or Bible, but we are promised guidance by the living contemporary Spirit.

(b) The theory breaks down entirely when we have to translate into languages other than English. How would you translate 'I am the true Vine' to the Eskimo or 'Behold, I stand at the door and knock' to the African native who lives in a hut and has never seen a door? The *truth* is indeed inspired but the *words* cannot be, if only because in innumerable cases there are no verbal equivalents in the hundreds of languages into which the Scriptures are translated. There is much in the Bible which is reasonable, but there is much in the New Testament which transcends human reason, but it is not therefore to be rejected. I think it was Weatherhead who said some years back, 'Faith does not contradict reason but it may transcend it'. I think he is perfectly right; Christians are not asked to believe what is clean contrary to reason, but they may be asked to believe in processes, laws and happenings which go beyond the present day limits of human reason.

There were many letters about details of translation, some referring to the New English Bible and some to his own translation. One which puzzled many correspondents, and left Jack pondering too, was the end of Matthew 5. Even though he persisted with his own translation, 'You are to be perfect as your Heavenly Father is perfect', he clearly preferred the NEB, 'You must therefore be all goodness'. To one correspondent he replied with an admission of his own concern about this translation:

Thank you for your full and interesting letter. Of course I had long ago recognized the difficulty of translating this word *teleious*! But what do you suggest? You surely cannot translate, 'Be ye therefore responsible as your Father in Heaven is responsible . . .' I suppose one could paraphrase and say something like, 'You must therefore be all-embracing as your Heavenly Father embraces all', but this is terribly clumsy. I thought I had partially solved the difficulty by saying, 'You are to be . . .' fairly translating from the Greek, I think, instead of the AV 'Be ye therefore . . .', thus avoiding the idea of instant perfection.

It is obvious to anyone who studies the New Testament that the true Christian teaching is one of learning and growth, e.g. 'Take my yoke upon you and learn of me', or 'not as though I had already attained or were already perfect'. Nevertheless, it appears to have been the ideal of Jesus that our aim should be the all-embracing love and compassion of our Heavenly Father. I personally like the NEB, 'You must therefore be all goodness'. After all, the standards of Christianity are indeed no less than perfection, but that does not mean to say that they are perfectly achieved in this life even by the saintliest.

Although seriously ill in 1961 he answered his letters and felt able to deal with a technical matter of translation:

> The word used is *koimontai* which is one of the New Testament words which can mean either 'sleeping' or 'dead'. For example, Luke 22.45 quite plainly means 'sleeping' and so does Acts 12.6. That the word was ambiguous is shown very clearly in John's Gospel chapter 11 verses 11 and 12, for here Jesus says, 'Our friend Lazarus sleepeth . . .' and a few words further on the disciples say, 'Lord, if he sleep he shall do well'. Further, the word cannot possibly always mean the sleep of death for in Matthew 28.13 the Roman soldiers are persuaded to say that 'his disciples stole him (away) while we slept'.
>
> Now when I came to translate 1 Corinthians 11.30 it seemed to me that careless participation in Holy Communion was not the cause of physical ills and certainly not of physical death. To my ~~mind~~ Paul was explaining to his converts that ~~careless~~ use of one of God's sacraments could cause spiritual debility and even death of the spiritual life. This still seems to me the force of the passage in question.

At the end of 1960, a letter arrived from Canada, raising a typical problem of translation:

> *I have for a long time wanted to ask you, whether the first verses of St John's first epistle could not be altered by the use of the personal pronouns. I have always thought Roman 8.16 — 'The Spirit itself' in the Authorized Version should be similarly amended. My knowledge of*

Greek is that of a schoolboy, who gave up learning in 1894! but I regard your books as paraphrases not translations — am I wrong? I much regret that your 'Preface' to The Young Churches *about the difference in the attitude to life of the writers and the present day, is not included in the complete New Testament, and wonder if you could have it included in future editions.*

He replied early in 1961:

May I answer your points in order:

1. I am afraid we cannot alter the first few verses of the first Letter of John. A neuter pronoun is used in the Greek, and John is really talking about the phenomenon which he has personally observed. Of course we know that the phenomenon was Christ himself. But that is not what he says in these particular verses.

2. In publishing the whole New Testament, I omitted all comment which might be thought tendentious or having a personal slant. This is in accord with other complete translations of the New Testament, such as Moffat, Goodspeed and the American RSV. The introductions to the various books are, however, retained in the Schools Edition.

3. Romans 8.16. Although the Greek word for 'spirit' is itself neuter, I felt so sure that Paul is speaking here and elsewhere of the personal Holy Spirit, that I considered myself justified in bringing in the word 'himself'.

Another correspondent, concerned about the translation of the word which is usually rendered 'commandments', wanted a word more in keeping with the graciousness of Jesus. J. B. Phillips replied with his views on this problem:

Thank you for your letter but what a task you set me! May I suggest that if you have a chance you look up the word 'commandment' in *Young's Analytical Concordance,* and you will see what I mean.

In general the word used in Greek is *entalma* or *entole*, both of which are derived from *entellomai*, which latter word means to enjoin, command or charge. This is a strong word, carrying the notion of authority, but naturally it has no flavour of dictatorial ferocity. Another word, which is used in Romans 16.26, 1 Timothy 1.1, and other places, is *epitage*, which means basically 'something which has been arranged'.

As for translating the word into English, I don't think you have very much choice. You can use 'order' or 'orders', or 'direction', but I don't think you can soften it any further. There are, after all, divine immutable principles which are as tough as steel. It is surely in the administration of these that God shows his great mercy to us sinners who bump up against them.

A few letters raised questions which were more human than theological, like this one from a school for deaf children:

> *I am wondering whether you can throw light on a detail of St Luke's account of the birth of John the Baptist which, although of little importance in itself, is of a particular interest to us here at this secondary school for deaf boys.*
>
> *Why (Luke 1.62) did they 'make signs' to Zacharias? According to the account he was deprived of the power of speech; there is no reference to loss of hearing. Is this simply a confusion of thought, or is there a deeper significance? And must we expect Luke himself to have been capable of such a confusion?*

Jack was particularly moved at the thought of helping a school for boys handicapped by deafness and he replied with care at once:

I think there is no doubt that Luke was a careful and accurate writer. Both his Gospel and the Acts bear strong evidence of being carefully compiled. I cannot therefore believe that he made a slip by saying that Zacharias was deaf as well as dumb until the birth of John. For myself I find the explanation in Luke 1.20, where Gabriel tells Zacharias that he shall 'live in silence and not be able to speak a word'. I don't see any point in the repetition of the AV, i.e. 'Thou shalt be dumb and not able to speak'. The Greek word *siopon* can easily mean 'hushed' or 'in quiet', so why not 'in silence'? That is why I have translated as I have.

Belief and Practice

Throughout his life Jack received letters asking for help with matters of belief and practice. A typical letter raised questions about 'the resurrection of the body and the virgin birth'. He answered this at length:

1. 'The resurrection of the body.' All religions, as far as I know, believe in some form of life after death, ranging from the 'Happy Hunting Grounds' of the Red Indians to the Nirvana of Buddhism. Christianity is concerned to express a belief in a personal resurrection comparable with that of Christ. Probably what Paul had in mind when he wrote to the Corinthians was (a) the Hades of both Greek mythology and the Sheol of Hebrew thought (both these states were pretty unhappy and insubstantial) and (b) the belief of some Greek philosophers of the immortality of the psyche but not of any body.

I think for Paul, as for us, words fail us when we try to explain anything which happens to us once we are outside the time-and-space set-up. We can only use picture language, and although I seriously doubt whether you are even approximately right in your molecular count of the entire universe, this is really quite irrelevant. In the life to come I doubt very much whether any present terrestrial physics has any bearing on the case; we are moving in a different dimension altogether. What is important for us to believe is that after death we do not persist as vague ghost-like creatures, nor are we doomed to lose identity in some fathomless sea of Being. For myself, I take quite literally the saying of Christ when he said, 'I go to prepare a place for you . . ., that where I am, there ye may be also' (*John 14.2-3*).

2. 'The Virgin Birth'. I do not think that this has ever been regarded as an essential part of Christian belief; certainly it could not have been in the very early Church, since it was not generally known. I happen to believe in it myself, after a great deal of thought, but I have several Christian friends who do not.

I think it is unwise to rest too much weight upon parallels with pagan belief to confute Christianity. Many religions provide parallels to such things as baptism, atonement, resurrection from death etc, but surely myths on which these beliefs are founded only indicate the projection of certain basic human longings. They are genuine longings to me; at any rate they are fulfilled historically in the Man Jesus, who was also the expression in human form of God.

Parthenogenesis, the technical name for virgin birth, is not at all rare in the animal world, but it becomes rarer as we ascend the scale of development. I remember hearing a geneticist lecturing on the curious effects upon animals by the very rare breakthrough of cosmic rays. Albinos in mammals are attributed to this cause. Only a year or two ago I heard a talk on television, again by a geneticist, in a science programme. The question of parthenogenesis came up again and the scientific speaker, upon being closely questioned, reiterated what I had heard before, that is, that the higher up the scale you get the less likely you are to find an instance of virgin birth. This was not, I would emphasize, a religious programme, but the interviewer asked, almost jokingly, how often such a phenomenon might be expected to appear among the higher mammals. The scientist replied quite seriously, 'not more than once in ten thousand years I should imagine'. I only mention these things to show that parthenogenesis is not impossible but only very, very unlikely. My own belief in the Virgin Birth rests on more theological grounds, and I would very much hesitate to limit the actions of God in his own universe.

A long letter from Canada about infant baptism received a very careful and lengthy reply:

The question you raise is, of course, one that has divided the churches for many hundreds of years. The whole idea of infant baptism dates back to primitive times when Christian parents whose lives were in imminent danger wanted to be sure that their children belonged to Christ. The early Church, as far as the records show, allowed this, provided that the child's promises were made by responsible adult Christians, that the child was instructed in the Christian faith, and later took on the promises himself in the rite of confirmation. This seems to have been the scheme of things in the main body of Christian practice. Of course it is open to abuse and godparents may be indifferent, and the child himself may not wish to be confirmed, etc.

My wife and I remember when our one and only daughter was born what a very natural and desirable thing it seemed to be that she should be 'baptized' or 'christened' and thereby made a member before witnesses of the church of which I am an ordained minister. To most Anglican (Episcopalian) thinking people there is no magic about the ceremony. It is an outward sign of God's love towards the child, but in another sense it is rather like a bank cheque. It doesn't really become of actual value until presented at the bank by the person in whose favour it is drawn. This, in the Church of England, is a rough parallel with our teaching about confirmation.

I have great sympathy with the Baptist point of view and with those churches like the Methodists who merely 'dedicate' a child in infancy and ratify this later with a ceremony comparable with confirmation. But I must confess I, myself, have no sympathy with the automatic view held by the Roman Catholic Church. To them the sacrament itself confers a special grace even if the godparents have no faith at all, and obviously the infant himself is not of an age to have something which might be called faith.

About the same time he dealt with a letter from a correspondent who was worried about the different denominations and wondered if it really mattered what you believed.

The trouble is that the existence of our various denominations is largely due to our varying interpretations of the New Testament words and texts. The extreme Anglo-Catholic regards the visible Church as God's instrument in establishing his kingdom, and he would claim that God marks his 'called-out' people by means of the sacraments. This seems to me manifestly untrue, since the Spirit of God is plainly at work outside any church and was given to the Gentiles at Caesarea while Peter was still speaking to them (Acts 10.44). And it is plain, to me at any rate, that the activity of the Holy Spirit is not confined to any particular church.

At the other end of the scale we find certain evangelical sects who believe that they are alone in being 'called-out' people. Church history shows that there has always been a tendency for certain Christians to become more and more exclusive, regarding themselves as the sole possessors of the true faith — a very dangerous thing to believe.

In Peter's first letter he states that just as the Jews were in a special sense God's people so Christians have inherited both the privilege and the responsibility of such a calling (1 Peter 2.9). Further, you will remember that in Paul's first letter to Corinth he reminds the Christians there that they are together the body of Christ, yet another definition of the Church (1 Cor. 12.27). I think therefore we should be very unwise to define the precise limits of the real Church here on earth. It may well be that there are those outside all organized religion who yet are in touch with the Spirit of Christ, and of course the reverse may also be true. I am sometimes haunted by 1 John 2.29, a text conveniently ignored by some evangelists!

A few months later he wrote dealing with a letter from someone troubled by the Jehovah's Witnesses and by pacifism:

I am indeed sorry that you have been worried by this sect calling themselves Jehovah's Witnesses. They are highly trained in manipulation of the Scriptures to suit their own particular purpose. But it is really unthinkable that all the Christian Churches throughout the world have been wrong all these centuries, and that this little sect should be right.

61

I have not the time to answer your letter fully, but there are two points I must make:

1. You will note that Jehovah's Witnesses deny the New Testament fact that Jesus Christ was God in human form (see Colossians 2.8-9 and many other places).

2. Over the question of war, which all Christians loathe, we are often faced in this life with a choice between two courses neither of which is absolutely right. I should say we are *not* right to fight for our own personal rights, but that we may well be right in fighting to defend other people.

Nevertheless, there are sincere Christian pacifists as well as sincere Christian non-pacifists, and both of them detest war. But there is no condemnation of the soldier as such in the New Testament. Indeed, in the Gospels and in the Acts of the Apostles centurions of the Roman army are highly praised (see Matthew 8.10 and Acts 10.1-2). If it were always wrong to use force, then no soldier and no policeman could ever be a Christian and evil men would commit more bloodshed than they do already.

Finally, would you please note that the commandment is 'Thou shalt do no murder' not 'Thou shalt not kill'. In other words, the individual must not take the law into his own hands but he has the right as a member of the state to defend, if called upon, the life and liberty of his fellow-countrymen.

The question of pacifism was frequently raised. In the next letter the subject has been brought up in relation to passages in *Making Men Whole* where J. B. Phillips had dealt with the love of God. He replied:

Believe me, I do appreciate your point of view, and I believe that ultimately no problem is permanently solved except by 'outgoing love'. But in this evil world there have to be interim solutions; for example, the policeman and the detective who protect the normal life of human society can hardly use the methods of outgoing love, as those words are generally understood, although of course they must at all times be just and merciful. There are many situations in life where the first step of outgoing love must be stern and uncompromising. May I ask you to consider what the Good Samaritan should have done if he had arrived on the scene half an hour earlier? Surely his outgoing love would have led him to defend the unfortunate traveller from the attack of the ruffians? It always seems to me the weakness of the pacifist position that while they are prepared to be Good Samaritans after the event they are not prepared to protect, forcibly if need be, the life and the liberty of the weak. In other words Peace is their God, and not the real God.

Jack was always ready to encourage youth groups and he was very pleased when after a broadcast, a leader of such a group wrote to him:

Our discussion which followed was very full and stimulating. We had submitted a question one week previous, and naturally examined your remarks in an attempt to gain your viewpoint. Could you, Sir, be kind enough to clarify for us your view on the following points?

1. You said that Christians cannot legislate for others! Does your remark here apply only to personal relationships, or is it intended to include the wider sphere of the community i.e. in Council Chamber or Parliament?

2. You said words to the effect that Christians should 'hold back' from expressing an opinion when 'expert' opinion is divided. On established issues such as the colour bar, cruelty to children, etc. we should speak clearly. By this line of approach, Sir, do we understand

*you to say that vital issues of the day must be settled
outside the sphere of the Church — that we in the
Church must just applaud when the matter has been
thrashed out?*

Such a letter was treated with great care:

It is good to hear of live discussion groups following
broadcasts such as we have been making recently.

May I briefly answer your queries.

1. What I actually said was: 'It is quite unrealistic for
Christians to legislate for non-Christians. The Christian
may, and indeed must, protest at what he knows is wrong,
but he must at all times realize that people cannot be
made good, or kind, or loving, or understanding, by force
of law.'

The sort of thing I had in mind is that you cannot make
people worship in church by closing cinemas on Sundays,
and the American experiment of prohibition showed for
all time that you cannot make teetotallers by law! But in
local government, by letters to newspapers and by every
legitimate means, the Christian should surely protest
against things which he knows for certain are morally
wrong, e.g. pornographic literature, sexually provocative
posters, and all sorts of social evils. The Christian, perhaps
more than anyone else, helps to form public opinion,
which in turn regulates the conduct of society. At the
same time it remains true that while evil may be
restrained, people are not converted by force of law.

2. On this point my words were these: 'I think he (the
Christian) would be wise to avoid hasty comment where
honest political opinion is divided, and where good
Christian men hold opposing views. But where he must
not be silent is where rights, human liberties and human

dignity are concerned. He must speak out, whatever the cost, and whatever the consequence.' Over the question of apartheid, racial discrimination, victimization in industry, and a host of other issues, Christians are often silent, and should to my mind speak out loud and clear.

Personal Problems

An increasing number of the letters J. B. Phillips received from readers were on matters of personal faith. Many of them were asking the very questions with which he himself was wrestling. Despite very considerable demands on his time, he was never too busy to deal with a troubled soul.

One correspondent wrote in appreciation of *New Testament Christianity* and then continued:

As I finished the book, I wished so much that I could talk to you because I have a great problem, one which grows with me always, and although I believe I shall eventually be helped to an answer or to an understanding, I wanted to put it down on paper: it would help. What if one has too much love? Or rather, if it seems impossible to use it all? It seems to me sometimes as much of a problem as not having enough. When I was little no one seemed to draw it out. As a young girl I suffered agonies in misplacing it; later I did find my husband, and he died; now a few years later, I have my son, five years old, and I have to be very strict with myself so as not to spoil him. I must not 'over love' him.

Every day and all day I steadfastly lay all this love, this reaching out towards every and anyone, before God. He knows that it all belongs to him, and he does give me some small opportunities for helping others, but it seems that most of this desire to love is wasted.

What is worse, is that I cannot resist the temptation to delude myself into 'loving' someone, a man, who is quite unworthy and belongs to someone else. I did not seek the temptation and was absolutely unprepared for it because I could never love any other man than my husband; but I was amazed, staggered at the pent-up feelings that this man has aroused.

I believe you will not mind me writing and telling you this.

He took time to reply with care and understanding:

One of the deepest forces in all of us is the desire to love and be loved. The form of this desire varies enormously with individuals, and of course with their upbringing and environment. In my experience people vary very considerably in, for example, the sex side of their nature. Some are almost born to be celibate, while others cannot really feel at peace without the satisfaction of married life. This is in no way their fault, since we have nothing to do with the construction of the glands which determine our sexual nature. But to anyone who is highly sexed and who has an affectionate nature life is never very easy if they cannot find proper fulfilment. The sensible thing to do is to recognize not only the forces of these deep God-implanted desires, but to realize also that by their very strength they can deceive us. For example, a girl may marry an entirely unsuitable man because her unconscious desire spreads a glamour over the man, at any rate before marriage. Similarly a man who has the mysterious power of awakening the opposite sex may create a false attractiveness around his own personality. Therefore, I think, we must allow the cold spray of reason to play upon the ardour of our feelings at times. In a sense we cannot have too much love, but we can have an affectionate nature which needs to be controlled and directed by reason.

It was sometimes difficult to deal with personal problems when they were presented to him from a distance and in a context he could not fully understand. One letter he received from a woman in great personal trouble was answered at some length but quite frankly.

I do appreciate your difficulties, but it seems to me that you are setting me a difficult, if not impossible task. One would have to know a great deal more than letters can convey, both from you and from your husband, before giving truly sound and Christian advice. Nevertheless it would seem to me that you are guided too much by feelings and impulse. After all, God has given us reasoning powers, and the cool streams of reason should be used to control the more fiery of our feelings.

I hope you will not feel that I am judging you harshly when I say that it seems strange to me that you say that your husband is a reasonable and reliable man and in the same breath you say you are convinced that he does not know the meaning of surrender to Christ. You are sorry for the 'self-righteousness and Christian rectitude' of those you left behind in England. But at the same time you do not find yourself able to exhibit the fruits of the Spirit, and confess yourself a poor example of a Christian. Now do not think I am blaming you, but there is surely something wrong here. It seems to me quite plain that there are adjustments to be made in your own personality — perhaps you have to learn to accept with more good humour yourself and your temperament, your husband and his temperament, as well as your family circumstances.

I would sincerely suggest that you seek the advice of

some trusted Christian friend with experience of dealing with human personality. He, or she, might be able to help you, first to let off steam and then to make the adjustment to life which, it seems to me, you find difficult. At this distance it is impossible to say whether this is a simple matter of a good laugh at yourself, or whether it is a longish business requiring patient Christian counselling. But you do need help, and you do need it, right there where you live. If I were you I should pray that you may be guided to such a person, and in the meantime try to pay little attention to your feelings and hold on to the facts. The fact is that God loves you unremittingly, and the fact is that God is within you, and the fact is that God wants you to become an integrated person. You haven't just to pull yourself together, but to co-operate with a Purpose already there.

To a question about divorce and the remarriage of divorced persons he sent a kindly pastoral reply which must have helped greatly:

My own view towards divorce, and that of my wife, is that it should be regarded by Christians as a very last resort. But, like war, it is sometimes the lesser of two evils. That is to say that because of human frailty and sin, the original divine intention about marriage is broken by divorce. Yet where the marriage has never truly existed, or where it has been 'murdered' by the behaviour of one or both of the partners, then it is better that it should be dissolved.

In my pastoral work I have sometimes, but very rarely, advised the dissolution of a marriage. Most of my work has been in the direction of teaching young people what marriage is and can become. And a good many hours have been spent in trying to repair relationships that have become strained or broken. I think the important passage to read is Matthew 19, particularly verses 10, 11 and 12. It seems to me quite plain that Christ was stating the divine principle, and also stating that not everyone had the gift to live up to this ideal. Not one of us is innocent in these matters, and if you feel in your heart that you are doing the right thing then you may be sure that God's blessing will be with you.

Often he recommended a correspondent to talk with his or her parish priest, but he agreed that this was not always appropriate, as in the following case:

Three years ago a new parish priest came to our church who is much 'higher church' than we have been used to before. We all liked him very much indeed: he is obviously a very sincere man. . . . He preached urgently on the need for cleansing oneself of one's sins before being in any way able to be born again and become a true Christian. He advised confession before a priest if one could do so willingly and sincerely.

I made my confession to him and somehow it all went wrong afterwards. Instead of feeling happier, freer, forgiven, I found it hard to face up to life at all. I lost confidence in myself — I became introspective and pretty miserable. I know now that I needed to talk my difficulties over with someone before I undertook what to me was a very severe task. Gradually during the past three years I have listened to many good sermons in church, I have read many books, I have learnt to pray, and I have come at last to understand something of the meaning of God's wonderful love and strength.

But always I find confessing intolerably difficult — it is not at all a happy thing for me — and when I read your book I at last thought that perhaps it is not meant for everyone — not for me?

But oh I do believe in the wonderful power of Christ's love in us — and I want now to live on this more positive approach of Christ's that you speak about.

He replied:

I would say first of all that confession to a priest is not meant for everyone. There is an old saying about it which runs, 'All may, some should, none must', and I should say that that expresses pretty well the mind of the Church of England on the subject.

I do not think it should be regarded as a duty, certainly not a regular duty, to confess one's sins to any other human being. Further, I know that human temperaments vary enormously. There are some to whom confession to a priest regularly would be a real hindrance in their spiritual growth because they would tend to depend more and more upon the priest's absolution and never enter into a real intimate relationship with God through Christ.

My advice therefore to you would be to discontinue confession to your priest. The thing that really matters is not whether his feelings are hurt or not, but whether you grow in knowledge and understanding of God. Many conscientious and sensitive people can have their guilty sense very readily over-stimulated. If you are one of these, as I suspect you may be, it is very much better, while sharing all your inmost thoughts and feelings with God, to let your mind feed upon the positive Good News contained in the New Testament. Notice, for example, how very rarely Jesus himself ever called people sinners. He called them rather to leave the past and its failures behind and to become the sons and daughters of God.

There is a favourite verse of mine which I think is especially meant for the sensitive and conscientious. It comes in 1 John 3.20 and runs, 'For if our heart condemn us, God is greater than our heart, and knoweth all things'. We may indeed through introspection grow to despise and hate ourselves, but God is greater and more generous than our petty selves and he is far more truly loving and understanding than we ever imagine. You cannot rest too much of your weight upon the real and contemporary God. I am quite certain that he does not want us to waste any time raking over our sins. He wants us to accept his forgiveness and walk forward confidently in his strength.

New Testament Christianity helped many people to understand the nature of faith in God and a section in it which dealt with the 'Love of God' continued to provoke questions for many years. Writing from a Canadian library where she had just read the book, one correspondent commented:

You say that we still have no clue as to the 'why' of our existence on this planet. That is the most baffling thing about life. Why are we here? If we are destined for a better spiritual life, why are we set on earth where everything wars against the spiritual? God made nature and so much of our nature leads us to unspiritual behaviour. Yet he wants us to be spiritual. Personally, although I am over forty I do not feel that I have ever achieved communion with God. The strange thing is that he does answer prayers when one is very worried or in a desperate situation, and yet the day by day or minute by minute contact seems impossible, except for saints. Parsons preach about prayer, but many do not seem much different from oneself, and you wonder if they have ever achieved it.

71

His reply is typical:

Of course I can't answer your main question; nobody can. We are in a difficult position on this planet, for the best of us walk by faith and not by sight. Just *why* God handicaps us so and yet draws us upwards to become like himself I really have no idea. I can only dimly surmise that we are somehow putting on spiritual muscle in the process, and that in a later existence this may be of further use in the great Purpose. I don't believe the wisest man could go much further than that.

It is difficult at this distance to advise you about communion with God. I am far from claiming that I achieve it constantly, or even daily. But I do know that it sometimes happens, and then so convincingly that there is no room left for problems or doubts. I think my rather unorthodox advice would be to seek earnestly with heart and mind the contemporary God, and then to think about something else! So long as we're pressing and straining, our personalities are too tight for the penetration of God. It is at the moments when we're off guard and relaxed that God will come sweeping in with his mystery and beauty. Even if we have no feelings of this kind for months on end, we can still regard God as a 'fixed point' by which to adjust ourselves mentally and emotionally. Good clear thinking in the imagined presence of God is, to my mind, true prayer.

A theological student raised problems that J. B. Phillips himself had faced and would face again:

I am still in a state of utter confusion. I try to push my doubts away and carry on, but it is nearly impossible to do so when the subject approaches every minute of the day. I have prayed, and it is my sincere desire to fulfill the will of God, and yet there seems no solution. So many things have to be taken on faith, and what can be done when that faith seems to be shattered? There are so many whys and ifs, and yet the need of God and Christian love in this world is so apparent. What can I do? How can I dare to proclaim God to others when such doubts exist in my own mind? If you can help me, please do, for I fail to see what I must do next. Will you please pray for me. God bless you and your work.

His answer:

My advice to you at the moment is to stop trying so hard. Relax your spirit and mind as much as possible. Read some books that have nothing to do with the Christian faith, see a funny film if you can. We are so constructed that if we keep on with a problem we tend to get more and more confused. Relax or divert the mechanism and give God a chance. Remember he will speak to you in non-religious as well as religious ways, and if you can bear it, he may be asking you at the moment not to take yourself so seriously! I know that you have to 'go through the motions' at college, but for the time being this is not hypocrisy so much as giving your mind a chance to recover its humour and balance. When you are able, try if you can, to see things 'from the angels' point of view'. Meanwhile, do remember that you're not the first or the last to go through a time of darkness and doubt.

Since I know there is a living God I am sure that he will bring you through it, but in the meantime don't over-dramatize the situation!

A very muddled correspondent from Scotland wrote to tell of her vision of her mother who had died, and of a friend who came to comfort her when she was near to death. Jack had had enough experience of this kind himself to take any person's visions seriously.

He replied like a good pastor:

> I don't in the least doubt the genuineness of your 'visitations', having had a similar experience myself. If we were not so preoccupied with this passing world, we should realize that the real indestructible world interpenetrates this one, and that is a source of comfort and inspiration in our earthly pilgrimage.
>
> I don't quite see why you draw a distinction between 'God' and 'Christ'! God became Christ at a certain point in history to reveal himself to mankind and according to the New Testament he is with us all the time. I doubt whether we mortals would be anything but overwhelmed by the slightest glimpse of the awe-full mystery of God, but seeing him focused in Christ we begin to understand his character.
>
> You cannot really 'make amendment for your sins' in the sense of making yourself right with God, as Paul tells us again and again in his letter to Rome. Christ has made the reconciliation and all we can do is gratefully to accept it, and live lives to prove that we appreciate his great love.

It was becoming clear to many readers of his books that, while J. B. Phillips wrote with the confidence of faith in God, he was not claiming absolute certainty for all Christian beliefs. He had said as much in *Your God is Too Small.* One correspondent complained that, if the evidence was as scanty as he said, was it sufficiently strong to carry the weight of Christian theology?

He replied with sympathy:

> I think I understand your difficulty, although it would

take a very long letter to explain what I believe to be true. I think Christians in the past have been inclined to overplay the strength of their position, and I have therefore been anxious to be fair. We do not know all the answers, nor have we such a vast weight of historical evidence as some might suppose. But I believe we have a real and genuine clue to existence, and sufficient historic evidence to make Christianity honestly tenable. We are, after all, dealing with the whole phenomenon of Christianity which cannot be lightly dismissed. No one would judge the size and value of an oak tree by the relative insignificance of the acorn. But the acorn is real and genuine and contains within it the potentiality of growing the oak.

Ultimately we do not solve the deepest problems of life by reason alone, or so I believe. If I plead for faith it is certainly not for an unreasonable or merely credulous act. I simply urge that in addition to using our rational faculties we also use instinct, intuition and imagination.

As late as 1976 he was guiding people in the spiritual pilgrimage and some words he had to say about prayer may make a good ending to this section:

I think it is important always to remember that when we pray 'in his name' we must of necessity mean 'according to his will'. I am often puzzled by what appears to be God's will, and often I can only pray rather feebly to meet it with courage, even when I haven't the slightest idea what he is trying to do with and through me. So I am a poor counsellor, I fear. But my heart and mind convince me that prayer, however imperfect, is never wasted.

After Jack's death some hand-written prayers were found which he had clearly composed for his own use:

Help me, my Father, to face life as it is, myself as I really am, and you as you really are.

Help me to see through illusion and not to be content with false values.

Help me to value the truly good things, to look for and see them, wherever they appear, and to thank you for them, for Christ's sake.

Give me an understanding and truly loving heart, my Father. Help me always to see people as your sons and daughters with personalities and rights that are sacred.

Help me never to assault or exploit or despise another and make me see the sin of such things, for Christ's sake.

Help me, O Lord, to keep a balanced mind. To enjoy myself, to recreate myself, to take every book or play or film as from you.

Help me to see that you are not only interested in the soul.

Help me to live, my Father, a day at a time.

Help me to rely on the abilities that you have given me and on the Spirit who is your great gift to me, and always to put your will first.

Help me to see the humour in things.

Help me not to be over-serious in some things or under-serious in others, for Christ's sake. Amen.

III

Sharing the Darkness

Much of this book so far has shown Jack Phillips helping others. We have seen how he sustained those whose faith had been shattered; but we have also seen another side. While some wrote to explain their dark shadows, he himself faced an inpenetrable darkness and cried out for comfort. The wounded healer was sorely wounded. His correspondence included, not only answers to those in need, but his own cries for help. Often when he read of healers who had experience of the darkness, he wrote to them.

An example of this type of letter is one to Michael Hollings:

> I only know you from the books of prayers which you have compiled with Etta Gullick, and you would know me, if at all, as a translator and Christian writer.
>
> Pages 145-6 in your book *The One Who Listens* describes the sort of desolation and darkness which I have tried to endure for something over ten years. . . .
>
> I can with difficulty endure the days but I frankly dread the nights. The second part of almost every night of my life is shot through with such mental pain, fear and horror that I frequently have to wake myself up in order to restore some sort of balance. If I don't manage to do that it quite often takes me three or four hours after waking to recover anything like a normal attitude towards life.
>
> My physical health is reasonably good. I have enough of this world's goods for all my needs and am not conscious of any particular unconfessed sins. I have a very wonderful

wife who stands by me steadfastly but I cannot help knowing that my almost continuous pain must be a burden to her. It is only during the last few weeks that I have been seriously assaulted by the thought that it isn't worth trying any more, I am too tired to make further effort and I really do not see the slightest ray of hope at the end of this very long tunnel. I think what chiefly worries me, apart from the sense of the loss of God, is the gradual failure of my own powers to love and be concerned about other people. It is true that perfect love casts out fear, but it is revoltingly true that constant fear and tension cast out love. All pain, especially of the mental kind, seems to me to make one more self-centred.

I don't know whether there is any word of encouragement or hope that you can give me, but since I am told you have had considerable experience with people in the dark places of life I feel it worth asking you.

The reply was very moving, but because much of it was personal it cannot be reproduced here. What can be said is that Jack found himself sharing the darkness with Michael Hollings, who paid tribute to his work and added:

Thank you for telling me. From my point of view, this will give me greater strength, because I can think of a person like yourself and share the burden. Thank you.

But as far as I know, the answer is that there is really only the way forward, which does not seem a way and which no one 'wants' to tread. There is no way out; *no escape which is more than a mirage, illusory. Go on. It has to be 'in faith' . . . and that faith 'in God', because human help whether medical, psychological or counselling fails. Unfortunately, only in the realm of faith does God not fail. It would be so comfortable to feel and know deep faith, but surely we can only live it and experience a darkness which makes everything else unreal. Be of good heart. The head is often useless and the heart is more clinging by love and trust than by conviction. I have always, in my believing life, been one who has if anything stressed the hardness and the Cross in the cost of discipleship. I do not see why it should not be laid heavily on you, because I have no doubt in my mind that God knows who he is taking up into the sharing of sacrifice. It would be lovely to stand outside and watch the wonderful way we were taking it, but this would not be to go through it.*

God alone knows how it helps and who it helps. But, again, I can just with the tip of my finger touch the sense that God can and does so trust us that he leaves us to shoulder the load in a way which is appropriate to us and to the world of our time. . . .

I think it is useless for you to wriggle on your cross; you are crucified there; accept it. The measure of God's love and trust is such that he treats you as he treated his own Son and does not have to pamper one who has served him so loyally and long.

Relax, he has you in his hand; there is no escape . . . and though there may not seem to be even courage to go on, he will lead you by the hand, invisibly, intangibly but surely on through darkness, until when he wills, you will see a great light.

In the poverty of my prayer I keep you. Now that I have written please keep me in yours, and the more difficult the better for we are dealing with Principalities and Powers.

That was to be the nature of the correspondence which Jack had with one Christian leader after another. He discovered he was not alone. Once he had taken upon himself to seek help he found companions also wrestling with principalities and powers, while the vast majority of those who read their writings or listened to their sermons thought of them as secure and untroubled in their faith.

Jack came to this state of sharing the darkness in three stages. Letters came to him about depression with no inkling of his own. Letters came from friends who had heard about his illness and sought to comfort him, but his replies often led them to reveal their troubled minds, or they volunteered a description of the darkness they had passed through in order to help him. Finally, in desperation he wrote to those who seemed to stand on secure ground, only to discover, that they too endured the suffering and darkness.

The night terrors continued; the paralyzing effects of depression ebbed and flowed like the waves of the sea, but never ceased. No easy solution came. In the dark experiences of his pain he could only repeat the words of Michael Hollings: 'There is no way *out*; only a way forward.'

The Unknown Helpers

Sometimes it was simply a letter of thanks which led him to respond with a description of the darkness. A woman who had been helped out of her depression by his translations wrote:

> *Time and again, during the past ten to a dozen years, as I have used your translation in my devotional reading, I have felt deep gratitude to you for the special enlightenments that touch my spirit. For years I had cherished the beauty of language of the King James Version of the*

82

Bible with a sort of 'religious devotion'. No other translation had ever brought satisfaction or challenge until, in a period of deep depressive need, I discovered your New Testament in Modern English. *Thank you for channelling the blessed truths in words that have given new life to them for me, and for others as well.*

Precious as passages of the King James still remain, the teaching and power that seems to flow through the pages of the Modern English version have brought me enrichment and strengths to sustain me in many a difficult hour.

I can't explain the compulsion I feel to write to you today. I want so very much to thank you personally for the peace that your great effort has often brought me — and for its challenge to my commitment. In the ups and downs of my life and spirit he becomes alive to me through those pages.

May the Lord who so helped you to bring his blessings and a knowledge of him to others bless you and yours mightily also.

She must have been surprised by the reply she received:

Thank you very much for your encouraging letter. You say that you 'can't explain the compulsion I felt to write to you today'. Well, I think I can! I am myself in the middle of a depressive illness and I have noticed that the good Lord seems to arrange matters so that I get a letter such as yours at a time when I have little sense of spiritual reality and am tempted to feel that my life is pretty useless.

For some reason I can't explain (although the psychiatrists would no doubt offer their convincing explanations) my own version of the New Testament doesn't help me at all in these days of darkness and I go back to the beloved King James Version.

I do not usually ask people directly to pray for me; but I do ask that if my name comes into their minds during their time of prayer they would remember me and my dear wife.

Some earlier correspondence was fuller. Jack seemed more able to tell of his troubles when he was seeking to help people see more clearly in the midst of their own darkness. After reading *Ring of Truth*, a woman gave her long case history. She described how she had cared for her husband who had had a series of strokes and then wrote of her own paralysis and loss of purpose. She ended:

But all my usefulness in home, parish and Deanery has gone. I can neither cook nor wash, nor sew nor garden, nor carry anything; nor play the organ or address Mothers' Union meetings; nor (most important of all) care for my still ailing husband. And now comes the awful thought — what if all my bright faith, my sure knowledge, has been illusion? Was the idea that my hands, feet, voice, intellect were being used by God just a piece of arrogant self-glorifying imagination? It certainly seems so now. I still believe implicitly in the Unseen — it's all around us — and in the Power that inhabits that Other World — the great Power that came down through Jesus, so that disease and death fled from his Presence. But that is the Jesus of history; where is the dear Christ of experience with whom I have walked and talked through the years? Life is so dreary without him, whereas before it was such a joyous thing! I suppose I shouldn't be bothering about it at seventy-nine — but it seems to matter now more than ever.

Please forgive me for troubling you in your busy life;

but some of the sentiments expressed in your book emboldened me to think that you might *understand and help me to 'get back'.*

Jack responded by sharing the darkness with her:

Sometimes one is tempted to the most dreadful self-pity and utter despair, but I have grown convinced that there is no way out along those lines! It would be difficult to summarize what I think God has been trying to teach me during these painful years. But one of the things I am sure is true is that *we must not* (as C. S. Lewis once wrote) 'lament over past raptures'. If we can look back and be *thankful* that we *were* useful, active and self-giving that is fine. But to look back and feel nothing but misery that we can no longer do what we once did is surely soul-destroying. I think our heavenly Father does not in the least mind a prolonged and violent grumble that this should have happened to us — we are, after all, only human beings — but he would be far better pleased if we took each day as it comes with courage and good cheer. With his help this can be done, though I would be the last person in the world to suggest that it is easy. But I remain convinced that the witness of people who are cruelly handicapped, or in constant pain, is as a matter of sober fact far more telling than the cheerful words of one who is in good health mentally and physically.

Perhaps almost the worst temptation when one is in the midst of this terrible darkness is to begin to think that all that we knew and felt, and almost saw, in happier days was only illusion. Of course it was no such thing. Do you imagine that Christ himself was not in an agony of doubt both in Gethsemane and on the cross? How cruelly he must have been tempted to believe that all that he had previously thought and proclaimed was no more than

85

self-delusion. I wish I could remember the source of a remark made by a great saint of God who emerged after many years from the kind of hell that you are going through now. She said, 'O God, where were you in all those terrible years?' And God replied, 'My child, I was there with you at every moment.' Without any question you will be told the same, whatever you may be feeling now. I can't explain this, I can only assure you that it is true. So do hold on and keep the flag flying; the King is still in residence.

Many of the later letters come from America. A woman in California had been greatly helped by reading the book *For This Day* which contains short extracts from the works of J. B. Phillips for each day of the year. She had recently suffered the shock of the suicide of her son and found the book comforting. She wrote of her trouble:

This book, plus a few others which I read around the same time, seemed to somehow permit me to accept extra amounts of the Great Comforter, which I was to need when my twenty-six year old son ended his life recently. We were not aware of all the pressures he felt — we were aware of many — but he could cope no longer and bowed out. He had had emotional problems for many years (schizophrenia). I feel that his healing will continue to completion now, and that ultimately we will share in the joys of the heavenly kingdom with him. I regret not having a good photograph of him, but such is the case; and our good memory of him the last time we saw him will grow into something more beautiful, perhaps as his resurrected life becomes more beautiful.

How wonderful you can write a book in England which can help a complete stranger half-way around the world in California.

He responded at once — telling her of his own pain:

I am sorry indeed to hear of the tragedy which you have suffered. But I rejoice that you have the faith to see beyond death and can accept that which I am sure is true, that the healing of your son will 'continue to completion'. For some years now I have been in continual pain, mostly centred in the eyes, and this certainly gives me fellow-feeling for those who suffer in this transitory life. The more one looks round on the world and the more one reads, the more one is conscious of the vast burden of suffering, both mental and physical, which afflicts mankind. Frankly I do not understand those who by their actions deliberately increase the burden. Life is hard enough for millions of people anyway without the added weight of evil inflicted by evil men.

It was kind of you to write. Some of my days are very hard to bear and it does cheer me a little (though it ought to cheer me a lot) to know that God uses my work in various parts of the English-speaking world to help fellow-Christians. I look forward to the day when mankind's burdens will be lifted and the love of God will restore and heal all men's wounds.

The answer delighted and saddened her at the same time:

I was delighted that you answered the letter that I wrote to you after my son's death. Friendship is what God's love is all about, and I feel that you are indeed, a friend.

I was saddened to learn of your continual pain, and wish there were some way I could help to alleviate it. I shared my concern for you with a few very close friends, and have asked that they join with me in prayer for you.

A man from Missouri wrote to him in 1980 when J. B. Phillips was himself suffering night terrors and feeling that the powers of evil were arrayed against him. His reply to the man seemed almost a word to himself:

> If I were you I should not think so much about the devil, but concentrate your thoughts and prayers upon our Saviour Jesus Christ. He will, without fail, defeat all attacks of the devil.
>
> The Christian life is a battle to many true believers, and it appears it will always be so. But the battle is one of *faith.* You, and I, must maintain constantly our faith in Jesus Christ. We then have nothing to fear from the enemy, however painful his assaults may be. If you look to Jesus and have his Spirit within you no devil can ever defeat you. I would recommend that you read your New Testament and especially Paul's letter to the Ephesians for help and comfort. God is always on your side.

It was probably in 1977 that he received from Canada a horrifying letter from a mother whose son had been sexually assaulted and as a result had become autistic. The mother was quite unable to understand the growing tolerance of homosexuality in churches. She trembled at the thought of what had been done to her son. No one could understand her violent despair and she turned to J. B. Phillips, whom she knew only through reading his books.

> *Now I turn to one who is in close communion with Him for encouragement — for help in combating what my whole being recoils from.*

It was a difficult letter to answer:

> I am honoured and indeed touched by your confidence in

me in telling me of your really dreadful tale of suffering. I have thought over your letter and its contents several times, and I cannot think of any way in which I can be of direct help. I can only reassure you that the words of the old negro spiritual, 'He's got the whole world in his hands', express a genuine spiritual truth. This world with all its evil, injustice and suffering is, whatever appearances may suggest, really in the hands of God. For his own good reasons he does not interfere during this present life. But I believe we can be sure of his ultimate triumph, including the righting of all wrongs and the healing of all injuries. This may well happen after what we call death and in a dimension outside what we call time. For the present I see no alternative for us who love and seek to follow Christ but to maintain our faith by every means available. I know nothing about autism except what I read and sometimes see on television. There has been a little, a very little, success in breaking through to autistic children. But some very skilled and devoted people are working on the problem. I most sincerely hope that things have improved in your part of the world since your horrifying experience some years ago. As regards homosexuality I am in a similar state of ignorance. I have never met a practising homo man or woman to my knowledge since I was ordained forty years ago. We are told that the condition is inborn and, though it can be controlled, it is only rarely completely cured. I have heard no official news that the Church of England accepts practising homosexuals as normal members of society. But I think it can, and does, offer any means of grace to those who are afflicted with this abnormality and who are sincerely trying to conquer it.

I don't think I can usefully say anything more. I find as I grow older life is more complex and puzzling than I had ever supposed. The forces of opposition are much more violent than I had ever seriously thought. I can only urge you *not* to lose the habit of prayer and *not* to lose your faith in the living God, whatever grievous errors the Church from time to time may commit.

May God bless and guard you.

Although the correspondence taxed his strength in times of weakness, it also encouraged him. There were many letters of deep appreciation. Others, like one that came in the midst of a very bad depression in 1967, allowed him to pour out his troubles. In the course of doing this he often told of how we hold on to our faith in desperate situations. This letter from a daughter of a Presbyterian minister and widow of a prominent psychiatrist with whom she had worked, intended simply to say thank you and share an amusing interpretation, but it hinted at a sorrow and loneliness that called forth his compassion.

She wrote:

Perhaps you would like to hear my interpretation of 'fear and trembling'. (It may give you a good laugh!) I remembered my precious cocker spaniels — one of which was my 'dearest friend', who, driving with me on several occasions across the USA alone, not only kept me company, but gave one real security. Lady — a golden cocker — would tremble in ecstasy, in anticipation of being allowed to go with me in the car — fearing, too, a possible denial, and most anxious to be near me at all times day and night, with every evidence of deep sympathy of my widely various moods, and a love which I keenly miss, even today! For love *has its various manifestations and while Lady became almost 'part-human' in her anxiety 'to keep in tune' with me, I became 'part-dog', in my efforts to bridge the gap — not as wide as some think! —*

between a loved animal and a desperately lonely human being!

He seemed on the right wave-length with this woman and wrote freely:

Thank you very much for your kind and appreciative letter. This is particularly encouraging to me because I have been 'under the weather' for the last few years and I cannot accept that at the age of sixty my work is finished! Unhappily I am drug-resistant to a ludicrous degree so that none of the psychotropic drugs produce anything but the most dreadful mental pain. I would very much like some of our experts who glibly write about their Monoamine Oxidase Inhibitors and the Imipramine drugs to be given a heavy dose themselves and then see what they say! The strange thing is that over the years, even with my somewhat elementary knowledge of psychiatry (which owed more to Jung than to Freud) I have been able to help quite a lot of people. Further my writings and broadcasts appear to bring faith and confidence to quite literally millions. My faith in God remains completely unshaken by the mental pain which is quite often excruciating, especially at night. All kinds of experts have given me such widely differing explanations that I cannot be blamed for being somewhat confused at times. I think perhaps the most helpful idea came out of a conversation with Harry Williams, Dean of Trinity College, Cambridge. He suggested that this is a kind of sharing in the sufferings of Christ, and is part of the price to be paid for being 'used of God'. When I can feel this I don't mind so much, but practically all the time, as in most cases of so-called 'depression', there is a total absence of the sense of God, and the diabolical suggestion that the whole thing, i.e. Christianity, is no more than a projection.

I assure you I don't believe this, and I am prepared to put up with a good deal of suffering. Many people do. . . .

I rather liked your interpretation of 'fear and trembling'! I am pretty certain that we shall all tremble with joy when we begin to see our Lord face to face.

There are many indications in the later letters of a growing tolerance with others who suffered. Moreover, some of the letters he wrote could not have been so helpful if he had not felt the pain himself. A man whose wife had committed suicide wrote in dark despair for this life and the next. Jack wrote out of his own sense of dependence upon his wife's love and care:

Thank you very much for your letter and for honouring me with your confidence. I am a little older than you and my wife is my best friend. I can therefore imagine how terribly lonely life would be without her and you have, believe me, my deepest sympathy. . . .

It is very natural and normal for anyone who suffers the shock of bereavement to blame himself. I am sure that you must not go on doing this. Only God knows what goes on in our hearts and minds and he alone knows how our minds will react to pain and stress. The very fact that your wife 'never complained' shows that she was repressing a good deal of emotion, and this she did, in my judgement, for your sake. We cannot ever know, in this life anyway, what a weight of agony led your wife to take her own life. But it looks as if she was a brave woman who was tormented beyond her capacity to endure. No amount of grieving on your part can alter this, and you really must make an effort not to brood over it. I am sure your wife would not wish you to do this.

I have a feeling that someone has told you that those who take their own lives are automatically condemned by the judgement of God. I do not believe that this is true. God 'who is rich in mercy' has a much more understanding and compassionate attitude to us poor human beings than our limited consciences will allow us to believe.

I do not think you need worry at all about seeing your wife again in the life that follows this one. It is obvious that you loved her deeply, and still do, and I would guess that she loved you too. This bond of love is not broken even by death.

The Fellowship of Suffering

Many letters that he received and to which he responded came from those who had heard of his suffering. The effect of hearing that one who had strengthened others was himself depressed brought forth some powerful confessions. One woman heard of his illness in a broadcast and wrote:

I did not know you had been so ill in the last few years, and so your testimony has all the more effectual power. And I am quite certain that this aspect is something we need to stress more than we do and gives more glory to God himself than any of the 'good works' of the Church. If I may speak personally for a moment, I have myself suffered a great deal in life, on the physical side, having had several severe illnesses, and finally polio some sixteen years ago, which has left me (fortunately) with a caliper and elbow sticks, but a rare complication of systemic gangrene set in about seven years ago and has made life slower and more complicated.

On the other side of life, I have had what most people would regard as a terribly lonely and unhappy childhood.

Then I saw my husband, a political refugee who had borne a great strain, change personality and become an utterly different sort of man with psychotic tendencies, a terrible persecution phobia and a really evil, suspicious mind! When I had polio, he couldn't take any more, and left me with three small children to bring up, and went off to Canada, where he presumably still is. The years of bringing up the children with no income, and unable to work, were very harsh indeed. But the dear Lord was with us always, and I have seen and known miracles worked by prayer, and told them to my friends, who have often found their own faith through knowing such things to happen, and, indeed, often, as it were, 'partaking in them', unawares!! I thought I knew a good deal about pain of all sorts, until my daughter, a nurse, had a car accident which she never bothered to tell anyone about and suffered from concussion and delayed shock, and tried to take an overdose three days after. In the next few weeks she made two more and very serious attempts to do it again, and finally for her protection I had to commit her for a month to a mental institution! It was terribly bewildering, as it was so much out of character with her normal attitude to life, until we realized about the bang on the head, and it linked up with her fiancé's death, two years before, who had been killed by a car. She is well now and perfectly recovered, happily married with a baby daughter they both 'adore'! But in the days I sat by her bed praying, and talking to her, I think part of my own life died in me, as though it had to go out a long, long way to find her spirit and bring it back, and was utterly exhausted after and still is very very tired! One can endure physical pain with the will, and one's own personal griefs and shocks, but to know another is suffering and you cannot 'communicate' is a terrible heart-breaking thing.

Yet, through all these things, and in, (because of, indeed)
all these things, I have never known God fail, and have
come to know him better, and trust him more fully than I
could ever have learned in happy ways and times. And
because his presence and his grace have been about me,
and worked behind and through all physical and mental
sufferings, one can bear the dark times of spiritual loss
and horror because the mind and the will know the
nature of his being and so can hold on and trust. By no
other thing than suffering do we learn to come into union
with Jesus more fully or more speedily. And to me, the
greatest value of any form of deprivation, etc. (quite apart
from and beyond one's spiritual life) is the wonderful way
in which it can be used by God. . . . People will not listen
truly to a fit person who tells them to offer pain to God
and try to rejoice in being able to share his suffering and
the burden of the world! But if they see oneself is crippled
and knows what pain is all the time, then they listen and
will think about it. . . .

I wish you'd write a book on the value of adversity and
the toughness of the Christian faith! I'm sure it would
help — and would especially help young people today.

That letter brought some understanding and allowed
Jack to say much more about his depression. She
responded with further letters.

I feel very honoured that you have told me of your own
personal trouble and I shall certainly remember you in
prayer in your great need and darkness. I know a little
how you feel — and especially the totally irrational sense
of terror which seems to swoop down and envelop one. I
think one is sharing at those times in the dereliction of
our Lord, who was 'bearing' the pain and terror and
helplessness of all those who through the centuries have

known terrible, inhuman agony and fear . . . all sorts of people in not only physical darkness and horror, but mental and spiritual anguish — the torn and broken spirits of all humanity through all ages. And in some sense, I believe (and I think modern psychology indicates this) that since all mind *is of common root, it is timeless, and we* can, *if we accept and endure,* be there *with those who suffered even centuries ago, upholding them in their agony . . . I think you will understand since you obviously know what your spiritual desolation is for. But may it not be a comfort to you to feel you are, by enduring with fortitude,* and love, *giving strength and comradeship to one who suffered (and is still suffering — where are we with words, and 'time', and past and present!) some terrible physical darkness and terror?*

One of the things I often wonder about is this — if Jesus shared our common nature in his incarnation, then he also shared that vast, uncharted evolving region of the collective unconscious which underlies us all — and at times threatens to invade and swamp us! *Such times of darkness and of special horror I think are such as you refer to.*

I shall remember your very real need in my prayers, for your spirit (let alone your human frame) must be stretched to its utmost on the cross. You won't *fail; you* won't *feel frustrated and give up, because God 'never suffers us to be tempted* above *what we are able to* endure!' *How that's comforted me at times!* He knows the breaking point and won't let us reach it, though we feel jolly near!! *May he bless you richly in all ways. P.S. I've just noticed you say 'I have not yet reached the point of realizing God is in this with me. . . .' But surely that is because he is so close to you? Not externally, so you can 'see' and 'touch', but you are* in *him and he 'in you'? That unity of being we desire of him and we do not always really grasp!! It's because you are so intertwined with his very being that you have lost the 'external' consciousness of 'Presence' — and you can't have closer union with him than that! You are a very lucky man, and have received what we are always praying for — but the price is pain — the pain and horror he himself knew!*

A close friend also reacted to the news of his suffering by telling of his own:

We were very sad about your set-back last week. What rotten luck! I wonder if my own experiences have any analagous features. . . . The strain, overwork and tensions of the war years resulted in my case in diabetes. It was also accompanied by a semi-breakdown mentally. I could not face the Plymouth office! We had just opened a day-a-week office in Launceston — my partners gave me permission to stay there full time, doing just as much work, or as little, as I chose. I couldn't face Plymouth people — either in the office or in the street. I avoided restaurants for lunch. I couldn't bear to go to professional and business dinners. I was, of course, terribly depressed. I had no physical pain, except an occasional discomfiture of unregulated diabetes. This went on for a year, but I began slowly to feel better. I realized however, that I could not go back to the pressure of the large Plymouth practice — so I retired from the partnership and operated the small Launceston practice. It meant financial loss, but I had the opportunity to work at my own pace. Almost every morning I would go to Launceston Parish Church for Communion, or Mattins and always meditation. But again the strain of rapid expansion was getting me down. I just had to get away from it. I decided to go to Theological College which I did in 1952/53. It was wonderful just to have the ordered life of an Oxford College without the slightest responsibility! The sabbatical year helped me to rethink things, and again my life was forcibly reduced to the pace that suited my health. At this juncture my human contacts were normal.

And I, of course, again made the mistake of taking on too much. Then one day in 1956 I went to Birmingham for a routine inspection of the Finance Company which was managed by my accountancy partner there. As soon as I started my routine check, he had a heart attack . . . I came back from Birmingham and just went to bed, hoping that I wouldn't wake up next morning. My doctor (and a specialist) gave me a check over. Physically OK apart from the diabetes, which was controlled anyway, but I had strict instructions that I should cut down the work. I remember asking if this really meant 'give up' and the answer was 'no' — go along at the pace you feel you can go and adjust according to how you feel. I mentioned that for some weeks I was so depressed that I didn't worry what happened to me. . . . Perhaps I may appear to you to be a self-contained confident unit, able to take what comes in life. In fact, I am conscious of the need for great spiritual support. I know that I must go on at a pace that is within my mental and physical strength. I have to avoid worry (how easy to advise — how hard to achieve!). Today I believe I am much better than I was a few years ago.

Now, there is, perhaps, not much in common with you. But there may be. I have bared my soul to you, as I have never done to anyone, in the hope that in my case history since 1946 you may see a reflection of yourself.

Particularly in the 1960s Jack found it helpful to be told by others and especially by his friends that they too had

been in the abyss and climbed out of it. Two letters —
written within a few weeks of each other — came from a
friend and colleague in publishing:

> *Your kind letter touches my heart and I'm so grateful.
> I'm slowly climbing out of the abyss of a nearly total
> nervous breakdown where the Prince of Darkness takes
> possession!!*
>
> *However by prayer and pills and the kind encourage-
> ment of J.B.P. I hope to prevail. Coming back to work is
> hell but it's the right thing.*

And then:

> *Since we spoke this morning I've been feeling that I
> ought to be able to help give you the reassurance you
> need. The fact that you seem to me to have had all the
> 'classic' symptoms of nervous tension and can, in fact, get
> despairing and frightened by them suggests to me that
> your will is, in fact, combating them. If you were in a
> state of suspended animation I'd be much* more *concerned
> about you. In practice (during the worst times) nobody
> will be able to give you comfort apart from medicinal
> relief from the irritating physical symptoms — the battle
> is only won by the patient himself and there is a great
> need to hang on to belief that long as the tunnel is, it
> comes out into daylight.*
>
> *I would hope you wouldn't take too seriously the charge
> of pride and self-congratulation for without those very
> qualities you could not possibly have achieved a task as
> great in our day as Gibbons (say) in his. To your friends
> you have* never *appeared in this light and now that you
> know you appeared (in these things or in this guise) to
> yourself* it can become a natural part of the wisdom and
> management of your own life — like the apparent

99

dilemma of puberty which loomed so large for many of us. I'll say it again — you have to go to the bottom before you can get up again and I believe (from our conversation) that the time of renewal for you is near. After four months of tears and terrors this year I have slowly got back my faculties and physical strength (with occasional set-backs) and I am facing all the problems quite well again.

May I say one other apparently irrelevant thing? Don't be afraid to spend money on some gay idea that suits you or your wife — in its own way that's an act of faith, a kind of throwing your biretta over the windmill of prudence. I bought my wife a new car when my reason told me I was a fool and it seemed to do something for me.

I do wish you better and know that you will be.

The Cry in the Dark

There were times when Jack received no comfort from those who sought to express their concern when they heard of his darkness by describing their own. Neither did the advice of friends who had been through the darkness help him in the long run. He knew that he had to face his own darkness and sometimes it was too much to bear. He tried many physicians and sought help as a voluntary patient in a psychiatric clinic. Always, the help went *from* him to others while little came back to him.

There were exceptions and they came unexpectedly. He would hear a broadcast or read a book or have news of someone who seemed to know what he was feeling. Then he would write — telling of his darkness and asking for help. Such an example was Harry Williams, who had written *The True Wilderness.* Surely he would understand and might help.

On 26 August 1965, Jack wrote:

I hope you will forgive a complete stranger writing to you, but I am somewhat at my wits' end. Although not entirely idle I seem to be going through the kind of experience which you describe in *The True Wilderness.* Indeed that book has been of tremendous help to me during some very dark days.

I am writing to ask you whether you could see me and possibly suggest a psychiatrist in London or elsewhere who could help me to make sense of what is happening. I may say that I have visited three leading psychiatrists in this area but none of them was able to give me more than superficial encouragement.

Soon after I was ordained in 1930 I underwent some psychiatric treatment from Dr Leonard Browne. All the insights I learned from him have proved true and, frankly, I thought I had got the whole thing licked. But what appears to be happening now seems to have no connection with the over-exacting father and the insecurity of a rather unhappy childhood which caused my former troubles. It feels as though demolition work were going on at a very deep level of the unconscious, and this results in quite irrational pains, fears and anxieties. I used to have dreams of an almost text-book clarity which served to warn me when I was straying off into the old paths of perfectionism, but nowadays there is no coherent dream but only a series of almost intolerably painful tensions which frequently wake me up in tears.

If you can help me, I should be most grateful.

Harry Williams met him and they liked each other. Jack gave him a copy of his latest book *Four Prophets* and signed it. This is his letter of thanks.

I am most greatful for your present. I want to display it prominently in my room so that people can see you've given it to me — but I have not given way to this ostentation. But I am delighted at your kind thought. Goodness, you make the prophets come alive. It's very frightening! I don't know whether you've seen the psychiatrist I recommended, or if you have, whether he is the right man for you. The personal equation is vital. He has helped me enormously but that doesn't mean he is necessarily right for you.

It is marvellous having met you. And thank you again for the book.

Jack evidently wrote at length to Harry Williams in 1968. Here is Harry Williams' reply:

11 June 1968
It was extremely good of you to write such a prompt and full answer to my letter. Naturally I wish you had better news of yourself. But I have known more than one person who six months or so after Electric Convulsive Therapy have been back permanently in their old form. I haven't had ECT myself, but I know you realize I understand the hell you are going through from my own experience.

I suppose what helped me most was the knowledge that Christ was helping some soul or other through allowing me to share a tiny fraction of his passion. This sounds horribly grand and good, but of course it wasn't really like that at all. I also cursed God and rebelled and pitied myself and so on in a very cowardly way.

What I think the church needs now is a renewed vision of the unseen world, and of God's saving power mightily at work, precisely while always bearing about in our body the dying of the Lord Jesus so that his life may flow out to the world.

Sorry, I am preaching of course to myself. For a long time I have been spiritually in the doldrums. Not alive but deadness and scepticism, a preacher without a message. Perhaps now the wind is beginning to blow a little. And it occurs to me that I possibly owe it to you. When the time comes I shall look forward enormously to your coming here. With many many thanks.

There was a mutual healing. The healing wind blew for Jack too — but only a little while. Then the darkness again.

For some time he carried on a correspondence with Leslie Weatherhead and this too started with a cry in the dark, as early as 1961. The correspondence reached an intensity of trust and understanding.

Leslie Weatherhead wrote:

I feel concerned about what you describe as depression because I went through hell thirty years ago. I had over two hundred hours of 'analysis' and finally emerged, but it took years. If there is any possible way I could help I would do anything I could. . . . Surely something can be done for you, who have done so much for others. I found Drynamil an enormous help to dispel early morning depression. These tablets are the basis of 'purple hearts', but in spite of all the talk about them, and their obvious dangers to foolish young people, under medical advice I think them invaluable. I still take one before a Sunday at the City Temple; a challenge which still makes me 'anxious'. Let me know if there is anything I can do.

Jack replied and Leslie Weatherhead expressed his desire to meet:

I wish we could talk! If ever you come this way come and have an hour or so. For we seem to have had so many similar experiences. Nowadays, I feel fine for weeks together and then there will come down a black cloud when I wish, quite sincerely, that I could die. I have thought so much about you but it would be presumptious to guess at causes in your case. I can only say briefly what happened to me in case anything in my case helps you. You have read the psychology doubtless. I was crushed between the super-ego and the id! I think success wrought my downfall, that is why I wondered if it might apply to you, a far more successful and famous man! Your name and fame are world wide.

I now look back and see this situation: I was a popular preacher, packing the City Temple, people queueing to get in, selling my books etc. etc. when all the time I knew myself inwardly to be a lover of applause! The conflict between what I pretended to be in the pulpit or at any rate thought to be, and what I really was, was too much and broke me in half. Could part of your trouble be the feeling that you don't deserve the praise of the whole world for your translations. You know they are jolly good. So were my sermons!! But human praise blows up the super-ego and makes bigger the contrast with the id, the gap widens when mental health demands they should be drawn together.

This may be no use at all, but I have noticed again and again, that in the very hour of triumph, when the whole world applauds, men suffer a 'breakdown'. The world's estimate and what a man knows is the truth make his mind split. Does this make sense? . . . My heart goes out to you because in some ways we seem to have been in the same dark valley. We shall emerge and we shall triumph, I am sure of that, if we endure to the end and soldier on as you say. . . .

Whatever happens in your mind you have wrought a

mighty work for the Kingdom of God. No one in your generation has done more. God bless you. You will find the way through and so shall I. May it be soon.

Jack replied:

Your letter was an enormous help to me! Not only have you gone up in my estimation by several hundreds per cent, but now I feel we are really communicating. Years ago at a Christian Books Exhibition in London you spoke to me most kindly, and I can remember saying to my wife and various friends afterwards, 'Here's a man who is just as friendly off the platform as he is on it!' And you know, as well as I do, that that is not always true of the world's greatest preachers. Through the years I have read all your books, and strangely enough the last one which you kindly sent me revealed to me more of you than it did of the Christian faith, if you see what I mean. But now that you have trusted me with such complete candour I feel I know you, and I shall certainly try to come and see you when I can.

There is a great deal of similarity in our experience of life. . . . What is so annoying about the present situation is that for twenty years, say from 1935-55, with the help of a most understanding wife who is quite the best human being I have ever met, I thought I had got the whole thing beaten. I did not realize quite how subtle continued success and being in demand everywhere could be. The trouble is, as you well know, that my talks, lectures, broadcasts and books were good, just as yours were. There is no temptation of this kind to produce an inflated image of oneself to a man who has no special gifts. But I found myself in possession of an embarrassing number of gifts.

I tell you all this because I know you will understand

that one can very easily think oneself, secretly at any rate, a kind of polymath. . . . It seemed I could do *anything!*

I came down here in 1955 (on advice of two bishops no less!) having built myself a house, and I used it as a quiet place for writing and a base for setting forth on Missions, lecture tours, broadcasts and the like. I kept the accelerator flat down on the floor, so to speak. Then quite suddenly, the creative urge was gone, and the colour and meaning drained out of life. It seemed to me as though everything was being knocked out of my hands. My capacity for affection almost completely disappeared and, worst of all, I lost all sense of 'God'. I don't think I ever seriously thought I had a 'hot line to Heaven', but there was always a definite someone (quite distinct from the father-image) to whom I could turn, and who was often consciously with me.

This, as you will understand, led to a situation of acute anxiety. Being fairly suddenly deprived of the ability to 'perform', my sense of security and of being useful deserted me and all kinds of nameless terrors swept over me, usually at night. There is no need to elaborate the physical symptoms because I'm sure you have experienced them all. I knew perfectly well why I felt insecure and afraid, but I could not see what I could do about it. No psychiatrist could tell me anything that I didn't know already, and, as I told you before, the psychotropic drugs did not seem to suit me, even in tiny doses. So I set myself down for what must be a long siege and so it has proved. Of course, the whole thing is irrational; these things always are. But that doesn't seem to stop the unconscious revving round at high speed, particularly when I am off guard in sleep.

Incidentally, although I have no intention of using LSD, the programme on BBC television the other night, particularly at the beginning, was an uncannily accurate representation of what happens to me without any LSD! The whirling colours, the visible sounds, the incredible speed of perception of all kinds fairly whizz through the brain. They are not terrifying in themselves in my case, indeed many of the designs are of extraordinary beauty. But it is alarming to have the brain working away like this without my being able to stop it.

I think the reason why Harry Williams' book, and he himself in person, helped me so much, is that he puts forward the suggestion that Jesus himself faced agonies and evils both at the temptation and in the Garden. He was not rescued, but he was given the strength to go through with it. Although I know no details I gather that H.W. himself has been through what he called 'sheer bloody hell'. And he offered me no pious platitudes but the strong encouragement of knowing that Christ went through something of this darkness himself, though for all I know it was infinitely deeper in quality. For the same reason, your telling me of your own experiences is far more help than any book of conventional pious comfort . . . I think, to be frank, that I can see the hand of God in all this. There will certainly be no VIPs in heaven and I think I can accept the fact that I am basically a perfectly ordinary person. To be made to realize this is terribly painful, because, as you know, the unconscious is thoroughly amoral and is determined to defend the status quo to the last. I don't think God minds hurting us in the least, but I am absolutely certain he will never harm us. There may be a chemical reason for this, or it may simply be that I have been, as one consultant put it 'scooped out' by continual demands. It may even be the assaults of the 'principalities and powers' who seem to be allowed to pick their targets. I simply do not know. But I am improving slowly and I have gained much greater insights than I had in the days of health and prosperity.

You yourself have helped so many people all over the world. I refuse to accept that your motives were quite so selfish as you make out; they were probably mixed like mine and most people's. Don't, I beg you turn against yourself. 'If our heart condemn us, God is greater than our heart and knoweth all things.'

It was a radio broadcast by Dr Weekes, which led Jack to embark on his final book. By now, he had more or less given up expecting much help for himself, but he thought an inside account might help others.

I realize that you will be inundated with letters after your splendid broadcast last night on *Living with One's Fears*.

I have had so much to do with this problem both pastorally and indeed personally during the last few years that your words were of extraordinary value to me.

Naturally I have ordered your book and expect to derive profit from it. I am not writing to ask you for medical advice (although it would be wonderful if we could meet) so much as to know whether you think it would be a good thing to begin an account from the inside, of what is popularly known as a 'breakdown'. I am a bit reluctant to do this but it might help others to know that a successful writer, in good health physically, can survive the real terrors and agonies which such a condition produces. Of course it would be better still if I could write the book after I had emerged from the depression.

That book became his autobiography, *The Price of Success*, which he left unfinished at his death in 1982.

Inevitably many of J. B. Phillips' letters included in the

third part of this book have sounded a note of brave endurance mixed with self-pity. But that was not the whole story, nor was it typical of the man. Ultimately he triumphed, retaining his faith and his sense of humour. As soon as someone turned to him in need, he forgot his own distress and gave help at once. Depressed he often was, but not in despair. If frequently he wondered 'what God was up to', and failed to find any meaning in the suffering, he nevertheless believed in God, and knew that his Almighty Father had a purpose, even though he could not always discern it, and that that purpose was good.

To the end of his life he continued to write letters of comfort and counsel, and to urge his readers, as he constantly reminded himself, to hold on to faith through all things.

These periods of spiritual dryness which every saint has known are the very times when your need of God is greatest. To worship him may or may not bring back the lost 'feeling', but your contact with God in prayer and praise will strengthen you spiritually, whether you feel it or not. . . . Times of spiritual apathy are the very times when we can do most to prove our love for God, and I have no doubt we bring most joy to his heart when we defy our feelings and act in spite of them.

If you give in to your 'feelings' you tend to become their slave, whether it is in the religious sphere or any other, and in any case you remain shockingly immature. The mature Christian gains his maturity largely by the exercise of his faith, and that means continuing to believe in God in spite of appearances and in spite of feelings. Give in to your feelings and you fall back; defy them and you may win a thrilling victory . . . and even if you don't, you have taken another step towards maturity.

What we need is continued courage and faith. If we are angry with God I'm sure he doesn't mind! To go on believing without knowing is what faith is all about. I will only say, don't lose your basic faith however much it is superficially scarred and pitted by this temporary life.

It is not so much our desperate attempts to hang on to God as God's unfailing will to 'keep us' that is so important.

As far as you can, and God knows how difficult this is, try to relax in and upon him. As far as my experience goes, to get even a breath of God's peace in the midst of pain is infinitely worth having.

It is much more than a crumb of comfort to know that whatever we feel, God knows all about it. Even when we find it next to impossible to pray, I am basically convinced that he understands this too.

I have been through prolonged periods of utter darkness and a good deal of mental pain and have by the grace of God won through.

1 Thessalonians 5.21: 'Hold fast that which is good.'